SpringerBriefs in Computer Science

AF670329

SpringerBriefs present concise summaries of cutting-edge research and practical applications across a wide spectrum of fields. Featuring compact volumes of 50 to 125 pages, the series covers a range of content from professional to academic.

Typical topics might include:

- A timely report of state-of-the art analytical techniques
- A bridge between new research results, as published in journal articles, and a contextual literature review
- A snapshot of a hot or emerging topic
- An in-depth case study or clinical example
- A presentation of core concepts that students must understand in order to make independent contributions.

Briefs allow authors to present their ideas and readers to absorb them with minimal time investment. Briefs will be published as part of Springer's eBook collection, with millions of users worldwide. In addition, Briefs will be available for individual print and electronic purchase. Briefs are characterized by fast, global electronic dissemination, standard publishing contracts, easy-to-use manuscript preparation and formatting guidelines, and expedited production schedules. We aim for publication 8–12 weeks after acceptance. Both solicited and unsolicited manuscripts are considered for publication in this series.

**Indexing: This series is indexed in Scopus, Ei-Compendex, and zbMATH **

Jiaming Pei · Lukun Wang · Minghui Dai

Federated Learning for Smart Mobility

Towards Secure, Efficient, and Sustainable Transportation System

Springer

Jiaming Pei
School of Computer Science
The University of Sydney
Sydney, NSW, Australia

Lukun Wang
School of Intelligent Equipment
Shandong University of Science
and Technology
Taian, Shandong, China

Minghui Dai
School of Computer Science
and Technology
Donghua University
Shanghai, China

ISSN 2191-5768 ISSN 2191-5776 (electronic)
SpringerBriefs in Computer Science
ISBN 978-981-95-6159-9 ISBN 978-981-95-6160-5 (eBook)
https://doi.org/10.1007/978-981-95-6160-5

© The Editor(s) (if applicable) and The Author(s), under exclusive license to Springer Nature Singapore Pte Ltd. 2026

This work is subject to copyright. All rights are solely and exclusively licensed by the Publisher, whether the whole or part of the material is concerned, specifically the rights of translation, reprinting, reuse of illustrations, recitation, broadcasting, reproduction on microfilms or in any other physical way, and transmission or information storage and retrieval, electronic adaptation, computer software, or by similar or dissimilar methodology now known or hereafter developed.
The use of general descriptive names, registered names, trademarks, service marks, etc. in this publication does not imply, even in the absence of a specific statement, that such names are exempt from the relevant protective laws and regulations and therefore free for general use.
The publisher, the authors and the editors are safe to assume that the advice and information in this book are believed to be true and accurate at the date of publication. Neither the publisher nor the authors or the editors give a warranty, expressed or implied, with respect to the material contained herein or for any errors or omissions that may have been made. The publisher remains neutral with regard to jurisdictional claims in published maps and institutional affiliations.

This Springer imprint is published by the registered company Springer Nature Singapore Pte Ltd.
The registered company address is: 152 Beach Road, #21-01/04 Gateway East, Singapore 189721, Singapore

If disposing of this product, please recycle the paper.

To all those passionate about intelligent and sustainable mobility, may this book inspire you to explore federated learning, embrace its challenges, and together, drive the future of transportation.

Preface

In recent years, the transportation industry has witnessed a paradigm shift driven by data, connectivity, and intelligence. As vehicles, sensors, and mobile devices continuously generate enormous volumes of data, the challenge of transforming this distributed information into collective intelligence has become a central research problem. Federated Learning has emerged as a promising solution to this challenge. By enabling collaborative model training without centralized data collection, FL provides a framework for privacy-preserving, distributed, and scalable machine learning. When combined with Internet of Things and edge computing technologies, it offers new opportunities to build secure, efficient, and sustainable transportation systems.

This book aims to provide a comprehensive introduction and analysis of how FL can reshape the future of intelligent transportation. The book is structured into five chapters. Chapter 1 introduces the motivation, background, and key concepts of federated learning in the context of intelligent transportation. Chapter 2 presents the theoretical and technical foundations, including FL architectures, optimization strategies, and IoT infrastructures that enable large-scale deployment. Chapter 3 explores practical applications of FL in smart mobility, covering autonomous driving, traffic prediction, and V2X security systems. Chapter 4 provides a comprehensive review of both academic research and industrial practices, highlighting lessons learned and empirical insights from real world implementations. Finally, Chap. 5 discusses the remaining technical, ethical, and policy-related challenges, and outlines future directions toward secure, efficient, and sustainable transportation systems. The intended audience of this book includes graduate students, academic researchers, and industry practitioners interested in machine learning, intelligent transportation, and privacy-preserving AI systems. The book seeks to bridge the gap between theoretical understanding and real-world deployment, serving as both an educational reference and a foundation for further innovation.

I would like to express my sincere gratitude to all colleagues, students, and collaborators who have contributed their insights to this growing field. Special thanks are also due to the reviewers and editors at Springer for their professional support during the preparation of this book.

Sydney, Australia
October 2025

Jiaming Pei

Acknowledgements This book would not have been possible without the support and collaboration of many colleagues and students. I am deeply grateful to my coauthors and collaborators whose work on federated learning, edge intelligence, and intelligent transportation systems has greatly inspired and shaped the ideas presented here.

I also wish to acknowledge the support from national and institutional research programs that have enabled the exploration of privacy-preserving and sustainable mobility technologies. My sincere thanks go to the reviewers and editors at Springer for their valuable feedback and professional guidance during the preparation of this book.

Finally, I am especially grateful to the members of my research group for their dedication and enthusiasm, and to my family for their patience and encouragement throughout this journey.

Sydney, Australia — Jiaming Pei
October 2025

Competing Interests The authors have no competing interests to declare that are relevant to the content of this manuscript.

Contents

Acronyms

AD	Autonomous Driving
AI	Artificial Intelligence
BRDL	Byzantine-Robust Distributed Learning
CCPA	California Consumer Privacy Act
CLL	Centralized Local Learning
CNN	Convolutional Neural Network
DFL	Peer-to-Peer Deep FL
DoS	Denial of Service
DP	Differential Privacy
EVs	Electric Vehicles
FADNet	Federated AD Network
FedAvg	Federated Averaging
FL	Federated Learning
FSD	Full Self-Driving
GD	Gradient Descent
GDPR	General Data Protection Regulation
GNNs	Graph Neural Networks
GRU	Gated Recurrent Units
HE	Homomorphic Encryption
IDS	Intrusion Detection System
IMU	Inertial Measurement Unit
IoT	Internet of Things
ITS	Intelligent Transportation Systems
LSTM	Long Short-Term Memory
MaaS	Mobility-as-a-Service
ML	Machine Learning
non-IID	Non-Independent and Identically Distributed
OBUs	On-Board Units
PeMS	Performance Measurement System
PFL	Personalized Federated Learning
PII	Personally Identifiable Information

ResBlock	Residual Blocks
RL	Reinforcement Learning
RNNs	Recurrent Neural Networks
RSU	Roadside Unit
RSUs	Roadside Units
SDGs	Sustainable Development Goals
SecAgg	Secure Aggregation
SFL	Server-Based FL
SGD	Stochastic Gradient Descent
SNR	Signal-to-Noise Ratio
TFP	Traffic Flow Prediction
V2E	Vehicle-to-Edge
V2I	Vehicle-to-Infrastructure
V2V	Vehicle-to-Vehicle
V2X	Vehicle-to-Everything
V-E-C	Vehicle-Edge-Cloud
VFL	Vehicular Federated Learning

Chapter 1
Introduction to Federated Learning for Smart Mobility

Abstract The integration of Federated Learning (FL) into smart mobility systems holds immense potential in addressing the challenges of privacy, security, and data decentralization in modern transportation networks. This chapter introduces the foundational concepts of FL, focusing on its application in smart mobility. It begins by discussing the motivation behind the digital transformation of the transportation sector, followed by an overview of smart mobility and its key components. The chapter then explores the primary challenges faced by data-centric mobility systems, including data silos, privacy concerns, communication latency, and energy consumption. The role of FL is examined as a natural solution to these challenges, highlighting its ability to facilitate decentralized data processing while maintaining data privacy. A typical FL architecture for smart mobility is also discussed, and an overview of the book's structure is provided.

Keywords FL · Smart mobility · Privacy · Data silos · Communication latency

1.1 Motivation and Background

The transportation sector is experiencing a profound shift, transitioning from traditional, infrastructure-based models to dynamic, data-driven ecosystems. This transformation is being propelled by the convergence of key technologies such as the Internet of Things (IoT), 5G connectivity, cloud computing, and Artificial Intelligence (AI) [25]. Today, vehicles are no longer just modes of transport; they have become sophisticated sensor hubs, equipped with cameras, LiDAR, radar, and GPS, generating vast amounts of data every day [9]. Simultaneously, transportation infrastructure is becoming increasingly intelligent, with smart traffic lights, roadside units (RSUs), and environmental sensors. The rise of connected devices is forming the backbone of smart mobility—a comprehensive framework aimed at creating transportation systems that are safer, more efficient, and environmentally sustainable.

© The Author(s), under exclusive license to Springer Nature Singapore Pte Ltd. 2026
J. Pei et al., *Federated Learning for Smart Mobility*, SpringerBriefs in Computer Science,
https://doi.org/10.1007/978-981-95-6160-5_1

At the heart of this transformation lies data-driven decision-making. The large-scale and diverse data streams from vehicles, infrastructure, and mobile users offer unprecedented opportunities to optimize mobility services. AI and Machine Learning (ML) models are employed to address complex challenges such as real-time traffic flow prediction (TFP), traffic signal optimization, autonomous driving (AD), personalized route recommendations, and vehicle maintenance predictions [34]. By analyzing both historical and real-time data, these models are able to identify patterns, predict future events, and enable proactive solutions. For instance, an intelligent transportation system can dynamically adjust traffic signal timings to alleviate congestion, guide autonomous vehicles through complex urban environments, or provide personalized travel suggestions that balance speed, cost, and environmental impact. These approaches are set to revolutionize urban mobility, significantly enhancing overall quality of life.

However, the success of these systems hinges on a well-integrated data environment—often referred to as the Smart Mobility Ecosystem. This ecosystem comprises four essential components: vehicles, infrastructure, cloud platforms, and people [6]. These elements engage in continuous data exchange, ensuring seamless interaction, as illustrated in Fig. 1.1. Vehicles gather detailed data about their state and surroundings, while roadside infrastructure monitors broader traffic conditions. Cloud platforms process large-scale data sets, and people contribute data through mobile applications, benefiting from the intelligent services provided by these systems. The synergy between these components is critical for unlocking the full potential of smart mobility, enabling cooperative vehicle perception, city-wide traffic optimization, and multi-modal transportation services.

Nevertheless, traditional AI models, which rely on centralized data collection, present several significant challenges in the context of smart mobility systems. In a centralized setup, raw data from various sources—such as vehicles and smartphones—must be sent to a central server or cloud platform for processing and

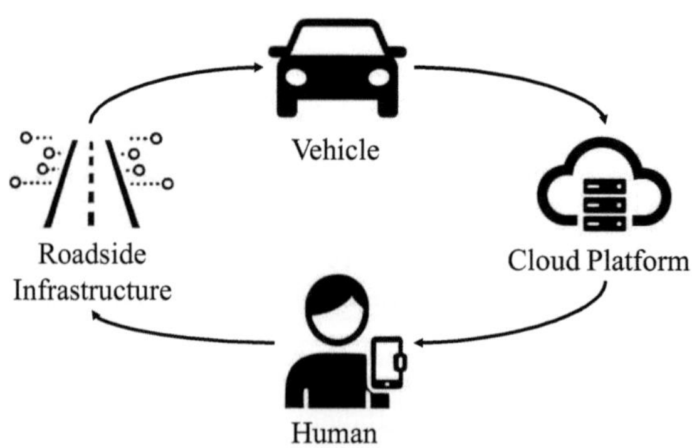

Fig. 1.1 A conceptual illustration of the smart mobility ecosystem, showcasing the interconnectedness between vehicles, roadside infrastructure, cloud platforms, and end-users

model training. While this approach has proven effective in many conventional applications, it poses several obstacles in the domain of smart mobility.

First and foremost, privacy and security are critical concerns. Mobility data often includes sensitive, personally identifiable information (PII) [28], such as precise location histories, driving behaviors, and even in-cabin video footage. Storing this data centrally creates an attractive target for cyberattacks, where a single breach could compromise the data of millions of individuals. As privacy concerns continue to rise, users are becoming increasingly reluctant to share their personal data. To ensure broad adoption of smart mobility services, a system that requires the sharing of private data may face substantial barriers to public trust.

In addition, regulatory challenges complicate the use of centralized systems. Laws such as the General Data Protection Regulation (GDPR) in Europe and the California Consumer Privacy Act (CCPA) impose stringent rules on the collection, processing, and cross-border transfer of personal data. These regulations often require explicit user consent and restrict how long data can be stored and shared. For global mobility service providers, navigating this complex legal landscape can be cumbersome and expensive, especially within a centralized data system.

Data silos further exacerbate the challenges of centralized systems. The smart mobility ecosystem involves a wide range of independent stakeholders, such as vehicle manufacturers, government agencies, infrastructure operators, and third-party app developers. Each entity generates and controls its own data, often viewing it as a competitive asset. As a result, there is little incentive for organizations to share their data, leading to isolated "data islands." This fragmentation prevents the development of collaborative AI models, hindering the creation of holistic, optimized transportation systems.

Finally, centralized models are limited by significant technical challenges. The sheer volume of data generated by vehicles and IoT devices makes it infeasible to transmit all this data to a central cloud for processing. This would place enormous strain on network bandwidth, incur high operational costs, and introduce latency, which is especially problematic for real-time applications such as AD [35], which require instant decision-making.

These challenges—ranging from privacy issues to technical inefficiencies—underscore the need for a new approach to AI in mobility systems. FL offers a promising solution [16, 22]. FL enables decentralized model training, where data remains on local devices and only model updates (such as gradients or weights) are shared for aggregation. This approach allows for the development of a global AI model while preserving data privacy. The difference between traditional centralized learning and FL is illustrated in Fig. 1.2. By bringing the model to the data rather than moving the data to the model, FL provides a scalable, secure, and privacy-preserving alternative for future transportation systems.

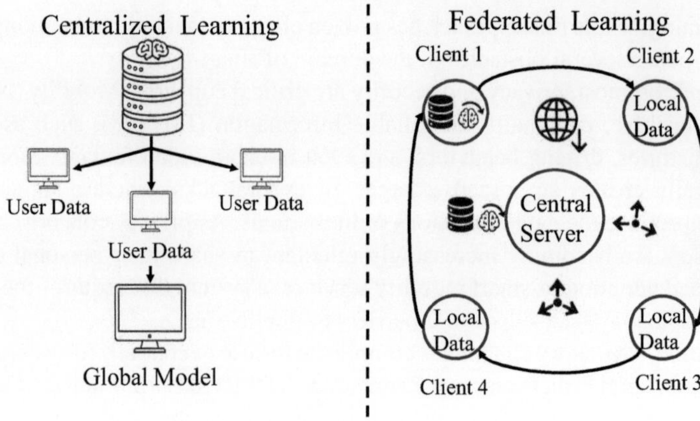

Fig. 1.2 A comparison between the Centralized AI approach, where all data is collected on a central server, and the FL approach, where data remains on local devices

1.2 Concept of Smart Mobility

Smart mobility represents a groundbreaking shift in the way we conceive transportation, envisioning a future where vehicles and infrastructure are seamlessly integrated into a user-centric, data-driven ecosystem. It moves beyond traditional models of transportation by transforming it into a more interconnected, efficient, safe, and sustainable system. The aim is not only to enhance existing transportation modes but to integrate them into a cohesive network that offers flexible, on-demand, and personalized travel experiences. This includes everything from real-time traffic management, autonomous vehicles, and integrated payment systems to shared mobility services like ride-hailing and bike-sharing. The ultimate objective is to optimize the movement of people and goods, reduce congestion, minimize environmental impact, and improve the quality of urban life.

This vision of smart mobility is built on four core pillars: **Connectivity**, **Intelligence**, **Security**, and **Sustainability**. These dimensions together create a comprehensive and adaptable transportation system that is ready to address the challenges of modern cities.

- **Connectivity** serves as the foundation of smart mobility [26]. Enabled by cutting-edge wireless technologies such as 5G, and the anticipated 6G, connectivity facilitates seamless communication between vehicles, infrastructure, pedestrians, and networks [21]. This constant flow of information enhances cooperative awareness, allowing vehicles to share sensor data and intentions with one another, which ultimately helps prevent collisions and optimize traffic flow. In a connected environment, each vehicle becomes an active participant in the broader transportation system, enabling real-time adjustments based on the state of the system.
- **Intelligence** powers the decision-making processes that drive the system [3]. By utilizing data from a network of connected devices, AI and ML algorithms analyze

and interpret vast amounts of information to improve traffic forecasting, optimize logistics in real-time, enable autonomous decision-making in self-driving cars, and provide personalized services tailored to user preferences. For instance, these algorithms can adjust traffic signals dynamically or suggest optimal travel routes to individual users, based on both historical and real-time data.

- **Security** is paramount to maintaining the integrity of the system [33]. As transportation systems become more interconnected, the risks of cyberattacks and data breaches increase. A robust security framework is essential to protect data, secure communication channels, and safeguard control systems from malicious threats. This includes the implementation of data privacy measures, secure software updates, and intrusion detection systems (IDS), all of which are critical for ensuring public trust and maintaining the safety of all users.
- **Sustainability** addresses the long-term environmental and societal impact of transportation [2]. This dimension emphasizes the importance of adopting electric vehicles (EVs), improving energy efficiency through smart charging and routing, reducing emissions, and encouraging the use of public transportation and shared mobility services. By focusing on sustainable practices, smart mobility not only enhances the efficiency of transportation systems but also contributes to the reduction of the environmental footprint of urban areas.

To support these pillars, the smart mobility ecosystem is structured into several interconnected layers, forming a sophisticated network of physical devices and computational resources. These layers consist of three main components: the **IoT and Terminal Layer**, the **Edge Computing Layer**, and the **Cloud Computing Layer** [18].

- **IoT and Terminal Layer** forms the foundational layer, consisting of a variety of endpoints that generate data. These include in-vehicle sensors (e.g., cameras, LiDAR), on-board units (OBUs) within vehicles, RSUs embedded in traffic infrastructure, environmental sensors, and personal mobile devices. These devices are responsible for gathering data from the physical environment and transmitting it to other layers for processing [7].
- **Edge Computing Layer** acts as a critical intermediary in the system [11]. It includes distributed nodes located closer to data sources—such as within the vehicle itself or roadside infrastructure. This layer handles time-sensitive and localized data processing, such as pre-processing, real-time analytics, and safety-critical applications like collision avoidance and pedestrian detection. By offloading these tasks to the edge, the system reduces the amount of data that needs to be sent to the cloud, thereby minimizing latency and bandwidth consumption, which is essential for real-time decision-making.
- **Cloud Computing Layer** sits at the top of the architecture [14]. It provides centralized computational power for more resource-intensive tasks, such as training AI models with large-scale historical data and performing city-wide traffic optimizations. The cloud is also responsible for long-term planning and non-real-time

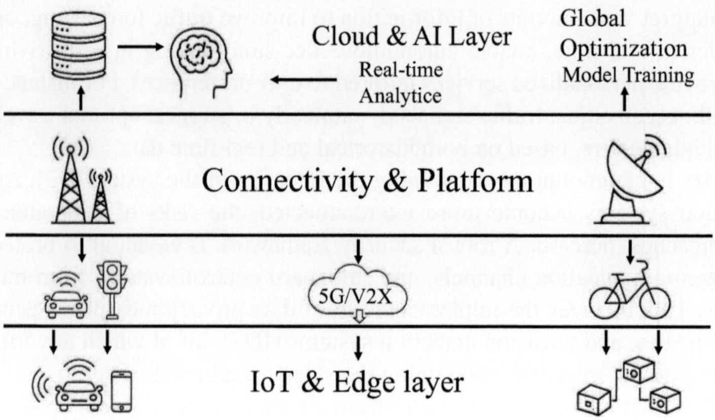

Fig. 1.3 The hierarchical architecture of the Smart Mobility Model, illustrating the relationship between the IoT/Terminal, Edge, and Cloud layers

services, such as updates to high-definition maps and personalized travel recommendations. This layer enables global optimization and supports large-scale data storage.

Together, these layers form the **Smart Mobility Model**, as shown in Fig. 1.3. In this model, data flows upward from the IoT layer to the Edge and Cloud for processing, while intelligence from cloud-based models is disseminated downwards to optimize traffic and guide real-time actions at the local level. This hierarchical structure ensures that smart mobility systems are scalable, resilient, and efficient, while also laying the groundwork for decentralized approaches such as **FL**.

In essence, the Smart Mobility Ecosystem represents a future-forward approach to transportation, where data and advanced technologies work together to improve mobility experiences for individuals while enhancing the overall efficiency and sustainability of urban environments.

1.3 Challenges in Data-Centric Mobility Systems

While the concept of a data-driven smart mobility ecosystem holds significant promise, its implementation faces a range of complex challenges. The very data that drives its intelligence introduces a web of technical, organizational, and ethical obstacles that must be overcome. These challenges are not merely incremental difficulties; they are fundamental issues that challenge the viability of traditional, centralized data management and AI approaches. Addressing these challenges effectively is essential to unlocking the full potential of smart mobility and ensuring its responsible and sustainable development. The key challenges can be categorized into four primary areas: **data silos and heterogeneity**, **privacy and security**, **communication latency and real-time constraints**, and **energy consumption**.

Data Silos and Heterogeneity

The landscape of smart mobility is inherently fragmented, with a diverse set of stakeholders such as vehicle manufacturers, public transport authorities, city governments, technology providers, and mobility service startups. Each of these entities operates independent systems and collects data for specific purposes, leading to the creation of massive, isolated **data silos** [36]. For instance, a vehicle manufacturer may collect detailed telematics and sensor data from its fleet but is unlikely to share this valuable proprietary information with competitors or even city planners. Similarly, a public transportation authority may gather rich data on passenger flows but may lack the tools or incentives to integrate it with data from ride-hailing services. This organizational fragmentation prevents the creation of a unified, holistic view of the transportation network, severely limiting the ability to optimize the system as a whole.

Compounding this issue is the challenge of **data heterogeneity**, which exists both within and across these silos. The data generated by various sources come with different characteristics:

- **Modality**: Data can be structured, such as telematics data (speed, acceleration), unstructured, such as video feeds from cameras, or semi-structured, such as point clouds from LiDAR and time-series data from road sensors.
- **Semantics**: Different systems may use varying definitions, formats, and standards for similar types of data. For example, one vehicle's perception system might label a "pedestrian" differently from another's, leading to inconsistencies during model training.
- **Quality and Granularity**: Data quality can vary significantly depending on sensor calibration, weather conditions, and network connectivity. The temporal and spatial granularity of data also varies, ranging from high-frequency sensor data to aggregated traffic counts on an hourly basis.

This heterogeneity makes data fusion and integration a challenging task [5, 17, 19]. It is difficult to train a single, robust AI model that can generalize well across such diverse and often incompatible datasets. Without mechanisms to bridge these data silos and harmonize heterogeneous data, the resulting intelligence remains localized and sub-optimal.

Privacy and Security Concerns

Privacy remains a top concern in smart mobility systems [12, 20]. Mobility data acts as a rich proxy for an individual's life, revealing personal habits, behavior patterns, and social interactions. Aggregating such data in a central repository creates an unacceptably high-risk profile, with a single breach potentially resulting in financial loss, safety risks, and a loss of public trust. The need for privacy preservation is underscored by an increasingly stringent global regulatory environment. For example, laws like GDPR [31] mandate "privacy by design" and "data minimization," meaning systems must be designed with privacy in mind from the outset, not as an afterthought.

Beyond privacy concerns, the security of the data-centric mobility system is a critical safety issue. As transportation systems become more interconnected, new vectors for cyberattacks emerge. Malicious actors may attempt to compromise the system in several ways:

- **Data Poisoning**: An attacker may inject malicious data into an AI model's training set [1]. For example, feeding manipulated images to a perception model could train it to ignore stop signs or misidentify emergency vehicles, potentially causing fatal consequences.
- **Evasion Attacks**: Adversarial inputs may be crafted to deceive a deployed AI model during inference [30]. A small, imperceptible sticker placed on a traffic sign could cause an autonomous vehicle's classifier to misinterpret it.
- **Denial of Service (DoS)**: Attackers could flood Vehicle-to-Everything (V2X) communication channels with junk data [8], disrupting safety-critical messages and disabling cooperative awareness features.

Ensuring the integrity, confidentiality, and availability of both data and AI models is not only a technical requirement but a fundamental pillar of transportation safety [23].

Communication Latency and Real-Time Constraints

The smart mobility ecosystem operates under strict real-time constraints, particularly in safety-critical applications. For example, an autonomous vehicle's decision to apply brakes or a traffic signal's command to clear an intersection for an approaching emergency vehicle must occur within milliseconds. The centralized AI model, which requires transmitting raw sensor data to a remote cloud for processing and then waiting for a response, is fundamentally incapable of meeting these low-latency demands [27].

The vast amount of data generated by modern connected vehicles—often exceeding several gigabytes per hour—creates a significant communication bottleneck. Transmitting such data over wireless networks is not only costly but also subject to congestion and variability, especially in densely populated urban areas. Even with the advent of 5G, delivering reliable, low-latency communication to millions of vehicles simultaneously remains a significant challenge [24]. The edge computing paradigm alleviates some of this pressure by processing data closer to the source, but it does not entirely resolve the core issue of how to collaboratively train a global intelligence model without overwhelming the network.

Energy Consumption and Sustainability

A final challenge is the energy footprint of the infrastructure supporting data collection, transmission, and computation. While smart mobility aims to reduce overall environmental impact, the processes of data streaming, storage, and model computation are highly energy-intensive [29]. The constant transmission of data from vehicles and IoT devices consumes battery power, which is a critical resource, particularly in EVs and battery-powered sensors.

Additionally, training large-scale AI models in centralized data centers requires significant electricity to power servers and cooling systems, contributing to a substantial carbon footprint [4]. This creates a paradox where the pursuit of efficiency through data-driven methods may lead to unsustainable energy consumption in the underlying digital infrastructure. To ensure that smart mobility is genuinely sustainable in the long term, energy-efficient algorithms and communication protocols must be developed.

These challenges—ranging from data fragmentation to energy demands—highlight the limitations of traditional centralized architectures. Collectively, they point to the need for a paradigm shift towards a more decentralized, privacy-preserving, and efficient intelligence model. The key challenges and their direct impacts are summarized in Table 1.1.

Table 1.1 Key challenges in the smart mobility data ecosystem and their impacts

Challenge	Impact
Data silos and heterogeneity	Inability to create a unified system view, leading to sub-optimal AI models with poor generalization. Limits collaboration and innovation across the ecosystem
Privacy and security	Increased risk of sensitive data exposure and breaches, undermining public trust. Vulnerabilities to adversarial attacks (e.g., data poisoning) that compromise safety
Communication latency and real-time constraints	Inability to meet the low-latency demands of safety-critical applications (e.g., AD, V2X). High bandwidth costs and network congestion issues
Energy consumption and sustainability	High energy consumption from continuous data transmission and model training. Significant carbon footprint from centralized data centers, potentially counteracting sustainability goals

1.4 The Role of FL

In response to the significant challenges of data silos, privacy, and efficiency inherent in centralized systems, FL emerges as a transformative ML paradigm [10]. It represents a fundamental shift in the approach to distributed intelligence, moving from the traditional "data-to-model" approach—where data is aggregated for training—to the "model-to-data" approach—where the model travels to the edge for training. This decentralized methodology provides a robust framework for collaborative ML without requiring the exchange of raw, sensitive data.

The core principle of FL is simple yet powerful. The process typically unfolds in a series of communication rounds, coordinated by a central server (or a hierarchy of servers):

1. **Initialization**: A central server initializes a global ML model (e.g., a neural network for object detection or traffic prediction) and distributes it to a multitude of participating clients, such as connected vehicles or mobile devices.
2. **Local Training**: Each client independently trains the received model on its own local data, ensuring that the data never leaves the device. For example, a vehicle would use its recent sensor readings to enhance a perception model, or a smartphone would use its location history to refine a route recommendation model. This step takes advantage of the latent computational power of edge devices.
3. **Model Update Transmission**: After local training for a predetermined number of epochs, each client calculates a model update. This update typically comprises learned model parameters (weights and biases) or their changes (gradients). Crucially, only this compact, anonymized model update is sent back to the server, not the voluminous and sensitive raw data.
4. **Secure Aggregation(SecAgg)**: The server receives updates from numerous clients and aggregates them to produce a refined global model. A foundational algorithm for this step is Federated Averaging (FedAvg) [15], where the server computes a weighted average of the client models' parameters. Advanced techniques like SecAgg can be employed to ensure that the server learns only the combined result, without knowledge of individual client contributions.
5. **Iteration**: The server distributes the newly refined global model back to the clients, and the process repeats.

Through these iterative rounds, the global model progressively improves, benefiting from the collective knowledge of the entire network, while maintaining data ownership, privacy, and locality.

FL as a Natural Fit for Smart Mobility

The unique characteristics of FL make it an exceptionally well-suited solution for the smart mobility ecosystem, directly addressing several key challenges outlined previously.

Privacy Preservation by Design: The most significant advantage of FL is its inherent support for data privacy. By keeping raw data localized on the end-user's device, it fundamentally minimizes the risks associated with data breaches, unauthorized access, and surveillance. This design aligns perfectly with the principles of data minimization and "privacy by design," as mandated by regulations like the GDPR [32]. For mobility service users, this means their location history, driving habits, and other personal data remain under their control, fostering greater trust and encouraging participation. While FL is not a panacea for all privacy threats (e.g., model inversion attacks), it provides a strong foundation that can be enhanced with cryptographic techniques like homomorphic encryption (HE), secure multi-party computation, and formal privacy guarantees like differential privacy (DP), which adds statistical noise to the updates to prevent inference of individual data points [37].

Breaking Down Data Silos for Multi-Source Collaboration: FL offers a neutral and secure platform for collaboration among competing or disparate entities [38]. It allows different vehicle manufacturers, each with proprietary datasets, to contribute to the training of a shared model. For example, a more robust perception model capable of detecting rare "long-tail" events on the road could be trained collaboratively. A Tesla and a Waymo vehicle, for instance, could both contribute learnings to a global model that is better at detecting a deer on a rural road at night, without sharing their raw sensor data. This collaborative approach dismantles the data silos that have traditionally hindered innovation, allowing the entire ecosystem to benefit from greater data diversity without compromising commercial interests or intellectual property.

Enhanced Efficiency and Real-Time Performance: Communication overhead is a significant bottleneck in data-centric mobility systems. FL drastically reduces this burden. Instead of transmitting terabytes of raw sensor data, each vehicle only needs to send a model update, which is typically orders of magnitude smaller [13]. This makes collaborative training over bandwidth-constrained wireless networks (such as 4G/5G) both practical and cost-effective. Furthermore, by pushing the training process to the edge, FL supports real-time adaptation. Models can be updated and refined locally based on immediate environmental conditions, enabling faster response times than a cloud-dependent system could achieve. This localized intelligence is crucial for applications like dynamic route adjustments based on real-time traffic or adapting a vehicle's driving style to local weather conditions.

Scalability and Personalization: The federated model is inherently scalable. It is designed to accommodate millions of participating devices without a proportional increase in central server load, as the most computationally intensive task—training—is distributed among the clients. This makes it ideal for the massive scale of IoT and connected vehicle ecosystems. Moreover, FL does not exclude personalization. While a powerful global model is learned collaboratively, it can serve as a strong baseline that is then fine-tuned or personalized on an individual vehicle or device. This hybrid approach allows users to benefit from both the collective intelligence of the network and a model uniquely adapted to their specific needs, preferences, and environments.

Typical FL Architecture in Smart Mobility

To effectively manage the scale and complexity of the transportation network, FL is often implemented within a hierarchical, three-tier architecture comprising vehicles, edge nodes, and the cloud. This structure optimizes communication and computation by introducing an intermediate layer for localized aggregation.

As depicted in Fig. 1.4, the process typically involves vehicles in a specific geographic area (e.g., a city block or a stretch of highway) sending their model updates not directly to a distant cloud but to a nearby **edge server**. This edge node, such as a Roadside Unit (RSU) or a 5G base station with computing capabilities, performs initial aggregation. It combines updates from its local cluster of vehicles to create an intermediate "edge model," which is refined more frequently and reflects local conditions more accurately. These pre-aggregated and refined edge models are then periodically sent to the central **cloud server**, which performs final global aggregation. The cloud aggregates the insights from all edge servers to produce the master global model. This hierarchical approach significantly reduces network traffic to the central cloud and allows for faster convergence of models tailored to specific local contexts, blending local responsiveness with global intelligence.

As a leading example, Google has successfully deployed FL at a large scale to improve its Gboard predictive text models on Android devices, demonstrating the real-world viability of this privacy-preserving approach. Similarly, automotive companies like Tesla, with vast fleets of connected vehicles, are perfectly positioned to leverage federated principles to continuously update and enhance their Autopilot and Full Self-Driving (FSD) capabilities by learning from real-world driving scenarios encountered by millions of drivers—all without infringing on their privacy.

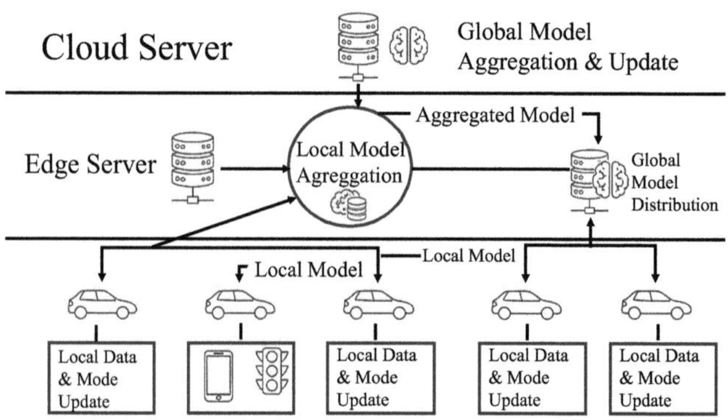

Fig. 1.4 A typical hierarchical FL architecture in a smart mobility context, showing local training on vehicles, intermediate aggregation at edge servers (RSUs), and final global model aggregation in the cloud

1.5 Book Structure Overview

This book is structured to provide a clear and comprehensive guide to the role of FL in smart mobility. The content is organized to build knowledge progressively, guiding the reader from foundational concepts and motivations to technical details, practical applications, real-world case studies, and future challenges and opportunities. The structure is designed to be accessible to a wide audience, including graduate students, academic researchers, and industry practitioners.

The introductory chapter, **Chapter 1, "Introduction to FL for Smart Mobility,"** sets the stage by introducing the digital transformation of the transportation sector and defining the core concepts of smart mobility. It then delves into the critical data-centric challenges, such as privacy risks, data silos, and communication bottlenecks, which hinder the progress of centralized AI systems. Finally, FL is introduced as a compelling solution, laying the groundwork for the subsequent chapters.

Building on this foundation, **Chapter 2, "Foundations of FL and IoT Systems,"** addresses the technical core of the subject by providing a thorough understanding of the essential technologies and principles. This chapter focuses on the "how" of FL, covering key architectures like horizontal and vertical learning, core algorithms such as FedAvg and its variants, and crucial privacy and security mechanisms such as DP and SecAgg. Additionally, the chapter explores the necessary IoT and edge computing infrastructures that form the physical and computational backbone for deploying FL in real-world mobility networks.

With the theoretical and technical groundwork laid, **Chapter 3, "FL Applications in Smart Mobility,"** transitions to practical applications. This chapter examines the "what" and "where" by showcasing the diverse applications of FL across the intelligent transportation landscape. We explore its use in enhancing AD through cooperative perception, improving TFP and intelligent signal control, enabling personalized route recommendations without compromising user privacy, and securing V2X networks against cyber threats. Each application is discussed to illustrate how the concepts from Chap. 2 are adapted to solve specific, real-world mobility challenges.

To provide empirical context and practical insights, **Chapter 4, "Case Studies and Research Insights,"** grounds the preceding discussions in tangible examples. This chapter synthesizes and analyzes a wide range of academic research and industrial implementations. It reviews key findings from published studies and examines how leading technology and automotive companies are leveraging federated principles in their products and services. A comparative analysis is presented, drawing valuable lessons, highlighting best practices, and offering a realistic assessment of the current state of FL deployment in the mobility sector, bridging the gap between academic research and industrial practice.

Finally, **Chapter 5, "Challenges and Future Directions,"** concludes the book with a forward-looking perspective. It summarizes the remaining open technical challenges in the field, such as statistical heterogeneity, communication efficiency, and model robustness. The chapter also explores the exciting potential of integrating

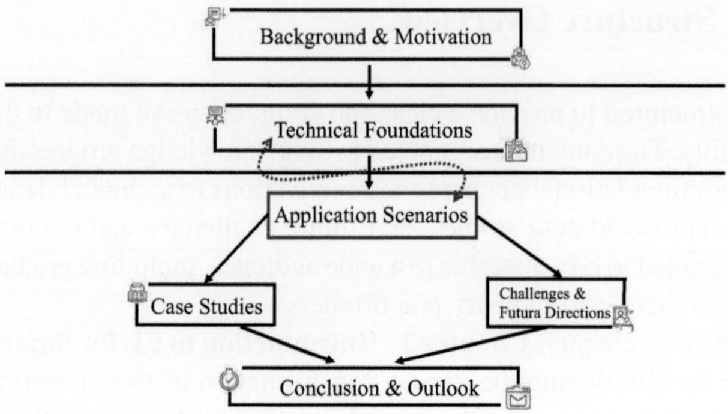

Fig. 1.5 A diagram illustrating the logical structure relationship between the five chapters of this book, progressing from motivation to future vision

FL with other emerging technological paradigms, such as blockchain, 6G communication, and digital twins. It concludes by addressing the policy, ethical, and standardization considerations that must be tackled and presents a long-term vision for a future where FL plays a key role in enabling secure, efficient, and truly sustainable transportation systems.

The logical flow and thematic connections between these chapters are visually summarized in Fig. 1.5.

Summary

This chapter has established the foundational context for applying FL to the domain of smart mobility. We began by defining the concept of a data-driven transportation ecosystem and immediately highlighted the critical challenges—data silos, privacy risks, and communication bottlenecks—that render traditional centralized AI models impractical and unsafe.

In response to these significant obstacles, we introduced FL as a decentralized paradigm. The core principle of training models directly on edge devices without sharing raw data was presented as a direct solution to the inherent problems of privacy and efficiency. By framing FL as the key enabling technology, this chapter provides the essential motivation for the technical deep-dive that follows. The groundwork laid here is crucial for understanding the core technologies discussed in Chap. 2, which in turn underpins the real-world applications explored later in this book.

References

1. Biggio, B., Nelson, B., Laskov, P.: Poisoning attacks against support vector machines (2012). arXiv:1206.6389
2. Biyik, C., Abareshi, A., Paz, A., Ruiz, R.A., Battarra, R., Rogers, C.D., Lizarraga, C.: Smart mobility adoption: a review of the literature. J. Open Innov. Technol. Market Complex. **7**(2), 146 (2021)
3. Colom, R., Karama, S., Jung, R.E., Haier, R.J.: Human intelligence and brain networks. Dialogues Clin. Neurosci. **12**(4), 489–501 (2010)
4. Dhar, P.: The Carbon Impact of Artificial Intelligence (2020)
5. El Faouzi, N.E., Leung, H., Kurian, A.: Data fusion in intelligent transportation systems: progress and challenges-a survey. Inf. Fusion **12**(1), 4–10 (2011)
6. Fantin Irudaya Raj, E., Appadurai, M.: Internet of things-based smart transportation system for smart cities. In: Intelligent Systems for Social Good: Theory and Practice, pp. 39–50. Springer, Berlin (2022)
7. Gokhale, P., Bhat, O., Bhat, S.: Introduction to IoT. Int. Adv. Res. J. Sci. Eng. Technol. **5**(1), 41–44 (2018)
8. Gu, Q., Liu, P.: Denial of service attacks. Handb. Comput. Netw. Distrib. Netw. Netw. Plann. Control Manag. New Trends Appl. **3**, 454–468 (2007)
9. Guevara, L., Auat Cheein, F.: The role of 5g technologies: challenges in smart cities and intelligent transportation systems. Sustainability **12**(16), 6469 (2020)
10. Kairouz, P., McMahan, H.B., Avent, B., Bellet, A., Bennis, M., Bhagoji, A.N., Bonawitz, K., Charles, Z., Cormode, G., Cummings, R., et al.: Advances and open problems in federated learning. Found. Trends® Mach. Learn. **14**(1–2), 1–210 (2021)
11. Khan, W.Z., Ahmed, E., Hakak, S., Yaqoob, I., Ahmed, A.: Edge computing: a survey. Future Gener. Comput. Syst. **97**, 219–235 (2019)
12. Li, J., Li, S., Cheng, L., Liu, Q., Pei, J., Wang, S.: Bsas: a blockchain-based trustworthy and privacy-preserving speed advisory system. IEEE Trans. Veh. Technol. **71**(11), 11421–11430 (2022)
13. Lim, W.Y.B., Luong, N.C., Hoang, D.T., Jiao, Y., Liang, Y.C., Yang, Q., Niyato, D., Miao, C.: Federated learning in mobile edge networks: a comprehensive survey. IEEE Commun. Surv. Tutorials **22**(3), 2031–2063 (2020)
14. Madupati, B.: Integration of cloud computing in smart cities: opportunities, challenges, and future direction paper. Challenges Future Dir. Pap. **06**, 2019) (2019)
15. McMahan, B., Moore, E., Ramage, D., Hampson, S., y Arcas, B.A.: Communication-efficient learning of deep networks from decentralized data. In: Artificial Intelligence and Statistics, PMLR, pp. 1273–1282 (2017)
16. Pei, J., Li, W.: Dual model pruning enables efficient federated learning in intelligent transportation systems. IEEE Trans. Intell. Transp. Syst. (2024)
17. Pei, J., Yu, Z., Li, J., Jan, M.A., Lakshmanna, K.: Tkagfl: a federated communication framework under data heterogeneity. IEEE Trans. Netw. Sci. Eng. **10**(5), 2651–2661 (2022)
18. Pei, J., Li, S., Yu, Z., Ho, L., Liu, W., Wang, L.: Federated learning encounters 6g wireless communication in the scenario of internet of things. IEEE Commun. Stan. Mag. **7**(1), 94–100 (2023)
19. Pei, J., Liu, W., Li, J., Wang, L., Liu, C.: A review of federated learning methods in heterogeneous scenarios. IEEE Trans. Consum. Electron. **70**(3), 5983–5999 (2024)
20. Pei, J., Xue, R., Liu, C., Wang, L.: Toward byzantine-resilient secure ai: a federated learning communication framework for 6g consumer electronics. IEEE Trans. Consum. Electron. **70**(3), 5719–5728 (2024)
21. Pei, J., Dai, M., Al-Dulaimi, A., Al-Rubaye, S., Mumtaz, S.: Task-oriented communication and optimization framework for 6g non-terrestrial networks: challenges and solutions. IEEE Commun. Mag. (2025a)
22. Pei, J., Omar, M., Al Dabel, M.M., Mumtaz, S., Liu, W.: Federated few-shot learning with intelligent transportation cross-regional adaptation. IEEE Trans. Intell. Transp. Syst. (2025b)

23. Pei, J., Wang, L., Awan, N., Alturki, R.: Advancing federated learning privacy with quantum communication techniques: a robust scalable framework. IEEE Syst. Man Cybern. Mag. **11**(2), 51–58 (2025)
24. Popovski, P.: Ultra-reliable communication in 5g wireless systems. In: 1st International Conference on 5G for Ubiquitous Connectivity, pp. 146–151. IEEE (2014)
25. Sadaf, M., Iqbal, Z., Javed, A.R., Saba, I., Krichen, M., Majeed, S., Raza, A.: Connected and automated vehicles: infrastructure, applications, security, critical challenges, and future aspects. Technologies **11**(5), 117 (2023)
26. Sethi, C., Singh, S., Raj, B.: Urban smart connectivity using intelligent technologies. In: Distributed Intelligent Circuits and Systems, World Scientific, pp. 111–152 (2024)
27. Shi, W., Cao, J., Zhang, Q., Li, Y., Xu, L.: Edge computing: vision and challenges. IEEE Internet Things J. **3**(5), 637–646 (2016)
28. Shokri, R., Shmatikov, V.: Privacy-preserving deep learning. In: Proceedings of the 22nd ACM SIGSAC Conference on Computer and Communications Security, pp. 1310–1321 (2015)
29. Strubell, E., Ganesh, A., McCallum, A.: Energy and policy considerations for modern deep learning research. Proc. AAAI Conf. Artif. Intell. **34**, 13693–13696 (2020)
30. Szegedy, C., Zaremba, W., Sutskever, I., Bruna, J., Erhan, D., Goodfellow, I., Fergus, R.: Intriguing properties of neural networks (2013). arXiv:1312.6199
31. Tankard, C.: What the gdpr means for businesses. Netw. Secur. **2016**(6), 5–8 (2016)
32. Truex, S., Baracaldo, N., Anwar, A., Steinke, T., Ludwig, H., Zhang, R., Zhou, Y.: A hybrid approach to privacy-preserving federated learning. In: Proceedings of the 12th ACM Workshop on Artificial Intelligence and Security, pp. 1–11 (2019)
33. Ullman, R.: Redefining security. In: Security Studies, pp. 11–17. Routledge (2011)
34. Veres, M., Moussa, M.: Deep learning for intelligent transportation systems: a survey of emerging trends. IEEE Trans. Intell. Transp. Syst. **21**(8), 3152–3168 (2019)
35. Wang, L., Xu, X., Pei, J.: Communication-efficient federated learning via dynamic sparsity: an adaptive pruning ratio based on weight importance. IEEE Trans. Cogn. Commun. Netw. (2025)
36. Wang, Y., Zeng, Z.: Data-Driven Solutions to Transportation Problems. Elsevier (2018)
37. Wei, K., Li, J., Ding, M., Ma, C., Yang, H.H., Farokhi, F., Jin, S., Quek, T.Q., Poor, H.V.: Federated learning with differential privacy: algorithms and performance analysis. IEEE Trans. Inf. Forensics Secur. **15**, 3454–3469 (2020)
38. Yang, Q., Liu, Y., Chen, T., Tong, Y.: Federated machine learning: concept and applications. ACM Trans. Intell. Syst. Technol. (TIST) **10**(2), 1–19 (2019)

Chapter 2
Foundations of FL and IoT Systems

Abstract Building on the foundational concepts introduced in Chap. 1, this chapter explores the core principles of FL and its integration with the IoT within smart mobility systems. The chapter begins by examining the different FL architectures, discussing their suitability for decentralized data processing in mobility environments. It then investigates optimization and communication strategies essential for improving FL performance in IoT networks, focusing on challenges related to resource constraints and network efficiency. Privacy and security concerns are addressed, emphasizing how FL can safeguard data privacy in mobility applications. The role of IoT and edge computing in facilitating FL is also discussed, highlighting their synergy in enabling real-time, localized processing. Finally, the chapter illustrates how the combination of FL and IoT enhances the scalability, efficiency, and security of mobility solutions, building towards a more connected and intelligent transportation system.

Keywords FL · IoT systems · Optimization · Communication strategies · Privacy · Security · Edge computing · Smart mobility · Data privacy

2.1 Overview of FL Architectures

As discussed in Chap. 1, the rapid growth of Intelligent Transportation Systems (ITS) has led to an increasing demand for efficient and privacy-preserving ML techniques. FL has emerged as a key solution, enabling distributed model training while maintaining data privacy and security [40, 43, 50]. By allowing multiple participants—such as vehicles, traffic management systems, and infrastructure providers—to collaborate without sharing sensitive data, FL has become a powerful tool in the context of smart mobility. This section provides an overview of the different FL architectures and their suitability for various ITS applications, as well as their implications for scalability, communication, and data management.

© The Author(s), under exclusive license to Springer Nature Singapore Pte Ltd. 2026
J. Pei et al., *Federated Learning for Smart Mobility*, SpringerBriefs in Computer Science,
https://doi.org/10.1007/978-981-95-6160-5_2

The architecture of FL can be broadly classified into three categories: Horizontal FL, Vertical FL, and Hybrid FL [36]. Each of these architectures is tailored to specific data distribution scenarios, and the choice of architecture depends on the nature of the data and the objectives of the collaborative learning task. This section delves into the unique characteristics of each architecture and examines their advantages, challenges, and potential applications in the context of ITS.

2.1.1 Horizontal FL

Horizontal FL, often referred to as Homogeneous FL, is applicable when participating entities share the same feature space. In ITS, this typically involves data that is structurally similar across vehicles or infrastructure elements. For example, vehicles from different manufacturers may collect the same types of data—such as speed, location, and acceleration—but store it locally rather than sharing it with others. Horizontal FL allows manufacturers to collaboratively train intelligent driving models using data from a wide range of vehicles, thereby improving model accuracy and robustness without compromising privacy [12, 41].

One of the key advantages of Horizontal FL is its simplicity and low computational cost, as the data is homogeneous across participants, making model updates relatively easy to aggregate. However, challenges arise when there are imbalances in data availability among participants. In cases where some participants have more extensive datasets, the resulting model may be biased, with updates from smaller datasets having less impact. Additionally, as the number of participants grows, communication costs increase because all model updates must be sent to a central server for aggregation. Centralized aggregation in Horizontal FL, although effective, can result in bottlenecks as the number of participants and the volume of updates grow, potentially reducing system efficiency.

2.1.2 Vertical FL

Vertical FL (or Heterogeneous FL) is applied when data across participants originate from different feature spaces but relate to the same sample space. In ITS, this often involves collaboration between systems that collect different types of data. For example, traffic management systems may collect data on traffic flow and road conditions, while vehicles (via V2X, or V2X networks) gather data on location, speed, and trajectories. Vertical FL enables these two types of data to be combined in the training process, facilitating applications such as traffic prediction, congestion management, and route planning [32, 42, 45, 56].

The primary benefit of Vertical FL is its ability to integrate heterogeneous data sources, enabling the development of more comprehensive and accurate models. However, this integration presents several challenges, including data preprocessing, alignment, and synchronization [54]. The diversity of data types can complicate the process of merging these datasets into a unified model, and the communication costs may be higher as the data needs to be exchanged between participants for synchronization. Vertical FL generally employs either decentralized or centralized aggregation strategies, depending on the system's requirements.

Vertical FL's ability to integrate diverse data sets makes it particularly valuable in smart mobility, where multiple types of data must be considered to optimize traffic management or vehicle operations. However, as with Horizontal FL, communication efficiency remains a critical challenge, especially in large-scale ITS applications where data flows are continuous and real-time processing is essential.

2.1.3 Hybrid FL

Hybrid FL combines elements of both Horizontal and Vertical FL, offering a flexible solution for more complex scenarios that require the integration of both homogeneous and heterogeneous data. This architecture is well-suited for smart mobility systems where diverse data sources need to be integrated to improve system performance [58]. For instance, data from vehicles (e.g., speed, location) can be combined with data from traffic management systems (e.g., signal timings, road conditions) to optimize routing, enhance traffic predictions, and improve safety.

The flexibility of Hybrid FL allows for dynamic integration of different types of data, adapting to the specific needs of each application. However, this flexibility comes at the cost of increased complexity in managing and processing both homogeneous and heterogeneous data. The system must also ensure effective communication and synchronization among participants, which becomes particularly challenging in large-scale systems that span multiple geographic regions. As Hybrid FL scales, careful management of communication and computational resources is necessary to maintain the efficiency of the system.

Hybrid FL holds significant promise for smart mobility systems, where large amounts of diverse data need to be aggregated in real-time. However, this architecture must balance the need for integration with the challenges of managing complex data streams and ensuring that the system remains scalable and efficient under varying communication conditions.

2.1.4 Aggregation Methods and Communication Models

The choice of aggregation method in FL has a significant impact on the performance and scalability of the system. Centralized aggregation, where a central server collects model updates from participants and aggregates them into a global model, is a simple and effective approach when data is evenly distributed. However, as the number of participants increases, the communication overhead can become a bottleneck, particularly when there are large numbers of participants or when network conditions fluctuate [47]. Moreover, the use of a central server introduces a single point of failure, which may compromise system reliability.

Decentralized aggregation offers a solution to these issues by distributing the aggregation task across the participants, thus improving fault tolerance and scalability [26, 44, 53]. In decentralized systems, participants communicate directly with one another to exchange model updates and synchronize their training processes. This approach can handle larger numbers of participants more efficiently, but it introduces additional complexity in communication management, especially in large-scale systems with wide geographic distribution. Furthermore, the lack of a central server makes it more challenging to coordinate and ensure consistent updates across the network.

In ITS, the choice of aggregation method can have significant implications for both performance and communication efficiency. Decentralized aggregation may be more suitable in environments where communication networks are unstable or prone to congestion, as it can reduce the dependency on a central server and improve robustness. However, as with all FL approaches, careful management of resources and communication strategies is essential to ensure the system remains efficient and scalable.

2.2 Optimization and Communication Strategies

FL enables distributed ML while maintaining data privacy, which is essential for applications such as ITS. As FL models scale and data heterogeneity increases, optimizing communication efficiency while maintaining model accuracy becomes crucial. This section examines key algorithms in FL, focusing on strategies that optimize communication overhead, address challenges related to communication costs, and balance these with model accuracy. Additionally, we explore how these strategies can address system heterogeneity and non-Independent and Identically Distributed (non-IID) data, alongside the role of client selection mechanisms in ITS deployments.

FL algorithms typically involve iterative communication between clients, such as vehicles or traffic management systems, and a central server. The server aggregates the model updates to improve the global model while preserving data privacy. However, as the number of participants grows and data becomes more heterogeneous, communication costs, data inconsistency, and convergence problems arise. Several optimization techniques and communication strategies have been developed to balance these trade-offs, ensuring both computational efficiency and model convergence.

Among the most widely adopted algorithms in FL are FedAvg [30], FedProx [29], FedOpt [48], and SCAFFOLD [22]. These algorithms are designed to tackle various challenges, such as communication efficiency, convergence under non-IID

Table 2.1 Comparison of Major FL Algorithms

Algorithm	Local update	Aggregation method	Proximal term	Optimization type
FedAvg	Local SGD	Weighted average	None	Basic
FedProx	Local SGD	Weighted average	Proximal regularization	Regularized
FedOpt	Adaptive SGD	Weighted average	None	Adaptive
SCAFFOLD	Local SGD	Control variates	None	Variance reduction

conditions, and minimizing the effects of system heterogeneity. Table 2.1 compares these algorithms and highlights their respective advantages.

2.2.1 *FedAvg: Federated Averaging Algorithm*

FedAvg is one of the simplest and most widely used algorithms in FL. In this approach, each client trains a local model using stochastic gradient descent (SGD) on its private data. After a predefined number of local iterations, the client sends the updated model to a central server, which aggregates the updates via a weighted average of the model parameters. The weighting is typically proportional to the size of each client's local dataset [30]. The raining and aggregation process are illustrated in Fig. 2.1, where the local model updates are combined at the server to form the global model. This simple yet effective approach has made FedAvg a popular choice for many FL applications.

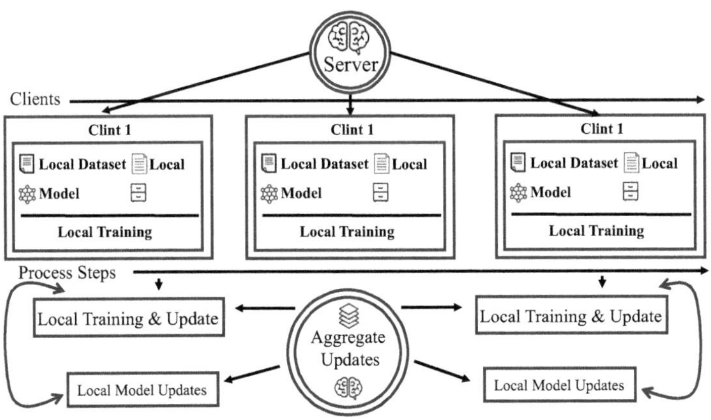

Fig. 2.1 Illustration of the FedAvg training and aggregation process

Mathematically, the global aggregation rule for FedAvg is:

$$w_{t+1} = \sum_{k=1}^{K} \frac{n_k}{n} w_t^k \tag{2.1}$$

where w_t^k represents the local model from client k at iteration t, n_k is the number of data samples on client k, and $n = \sum_{k=1}^{K} n_k$ is the total number of samples across all clients. This weighted aggregation ensures proportional contributions from each client [30].

FedAvg, while efficient for many scenarios, struggles with non-IID data distributions. In cases where data across clients is highly heterogeneous, the aggregated model may fail to generalize well, leading to suboptimal performance.

2.2.2 FedProx: Federated Proximal Algorithm

FedProx [29] addresses the challenges posed by non-IID data by incorporating a proximal regularization term into the local optimization objective. This regularization penalizes large deviations between the local models and the global model, improving stability and convergence.

The local optimization problem for each client in FedProx is formulated as:

$$\min_{w} f_k(w) + \frac{\mu}{2} \|w - w_t\|^2 \tag{2.2}$$

where $f_k(w)$ is the local loss function, w_t is the global model, and μ is a regularization parameter [29]. The inclusion of the proximal term ensures that the local models do not deviate too far from the global model, thus stabilizing training under heterogeneous conditions.

FedProx is particularly useful in scenarios where data variability across clients is significant, such as vehicles equipped with different sensors or traffic management systems with varying data types.

2.2.3 FedOpt: Federated Optimization Algorithm

FedOpt [48] builds on FedAvg by introducing adaptive optimization techniques. These optimizers, such as Adam or Adagrad, adjust the learning rate based on the gradients, allowing for faster convergence and improved robustness to fluctuating communication conditions.

The global model update rule in FedOpt is:

$$w_{t+1} = w_t - \eta_t \cdot \text{Opt}\left(\sum_{k=1}^{K} \frac{n_k}{n}(w_t - w_t^k)\right) \tag{2.3}$$

where Opt(·) represents an adaptive optimizer (e.g., Adam), and η_t is the adaptive learning rate [48]. By leveraging adaptive gradients, FedOpt improves convergence speed, especially in environments with communication instability, making it a suitable choice for vehicular networks or dynamic ITS environments.

2.2.4 Communication Efficiency Strategies

One of the critical challenges in FL is communication efficiency. The transmission of model updates can incur high bandwidth costs, especially when the number of clients is large or the models are complex. Several strategies have been proposed to mitigate this issue, including client sampling, asynchronous updates, and compression techniques.

Client sampling reduces communication overhead by randomly selecting a subset of clients to participate in each training round [13]. This method is especially beneficial in large-scale systems like ITS, where it is impractical to involve all clients in every round. Care must be taken to ensure that the selected clients are representative of the overall dataset, maintaining the diversity of the data while reducing the communication load.

Asynchronous updates enable clients to send their updates as soon as they finish their local training, instead of waiting for all clients to complete their updates. This approach speeds up the training process and reduces latency [31]. The update rule for asynchronous updates is:

$$w_{t+1} = (1 - \alpha_t)w_t + \alpha_t w_t^k \tag{2.4}$$

where α_t is a dynamic weighting factor that adjusts the influence of each asynchronous update.

Compression techniques such as quantization and sparsification reduce the size of the model updates. Sparsification, for example, retains only the most significant components of the model update [4]:

$$\tilde{g}_t^k = \mathcal{S}_\theta(g_t^k) \tag{2.5}$$

where $\mathcal{S}_\theta(\cdot)$ is the sparsification operator that keeps only the top-$\theta\%$ largest gradient components.

2.2.5 *Client Selection Strategies*

Client selection is a critical aspect of FL. Random selection may lead to biased updates, as some clients may disproportionately influence the global model. To improve model accuracy and representativeness, importance sampling can be employed, where clients are selected based on the relevance of their data [21]:

$$p_k = \frac{q_k}{\sum_{i=1}^{K} q_i} \tag{2.6}$$

where q_k is the importance score for client k, reflecting the relevance or diversity of the client's data.

2.3 FL in ITS

FL plays a key role in enabling collaborative model training in ITS without the need to share sensitive data [46]. In an ITS environment, vehicles and infrastructure collectively contribute to model training, ensuring privacy while benefiting from shared knowledge. The global model update in ITS is given by:

$$w_{t+1}^{ITS} = \sum_{v \in \mathcal{V}} \frac{n_v}{n} w_t^v \tag{2.7}$$

where $\mathcal{V}$ represents the set of participating vehicles, and w_t^v is the model update from each vehicle [24]. This collaborative approach allows for real-time adaptation of models, such as those for traffic prediction and route optimization, while preserving the privacy of individual vehicles' data.

2.4 Privacy and Security Mechanisms

As FL continues to be a popular paradigm for decentralized ML, it presents several challenges related to privacy and security. In federated settings, raw data remains on client devices, which is beneficial for privacy but creates new vulnerabilities. The main concern is that during the process of aggregating model updates across devices, private information might still be exposed [20]. The goal is therefore to ensure that the shared model parameters $\mathbf{w}_i^t$ or their gradients $\nabla \mathcal{L}_i(\mathbf{w}_i^t)$ do not leak sensitive information from local datasets D_i.

This section delves into the key privacy and security mechanisms designed to protect sensitive information in FL: DP, SecAgg, and HE. Additionally, we will discuss common attacks, defenses, and the trade-offs between privacy protection and model performance, which are especially crucial in dynamic environments such as ITS.

Differential Privacy:

DP provides formal privacy guarantees [15] by ensuring that an individual's data cannot be inferred from the output of a computation, even when an adversary has access to other parts of the dataset. The goal of DP is to make it impossible for anyone observing the output of a model to infer whether any specific individual's data was included in the training process. The key idea is to add random noise to the model updates or gradients, making it difficult to reverse-engineer the original data.

Formally, a randomized mechanism M satisfies (ϵ, δ)-DP if, for any two datasets D and D' that differ by one sample, the following holds:

$$\mathbb{P}[M(D) \in S] \leq e^{\epsilon} \cdot \mathbb{P}[M(D') \in S] + \delta, \quad \forall S \subseteq \mathcal{Z} \tag{2.8}$$

where ϵ is the privacy budget (controlling the strength of privacy) and δ is the tolerance for privacy leakage.

In practice, the FL client adds Gaussian noise to its local model update [2] before uploading (Fig. 2.2).

$$\tilde{\mathbf{w}}_i^t = \mathbf{w}_i^t + \mathcal{N}(0, \sigma^2 I) \tag{2.9}$$

where σ determines the magnitude of the noise. The larger σ, the stronger the privacy protection, but the greater the impact on model accuracy. The variance σ^2 is typically derived from the desired ϵ-DP level:

$$\sigma^2 \geq \frac{2\ln(1.25/\delta)}{\epsilon^2}\Delta^2 \tag{2.10}$$

where Δ denotes the sensitivity of the update function (i.e., the maximum change in output caused by modifying one sample).

In FL, DP ensures that each client's contribution remains indistinguishable, but excessive noise can slow convergence or degrade prediction accuracy. Hence, DP must balance the trade-off between privacy (ϵ) and utility (accuracy), which is often adjusted dynamically across rounds.

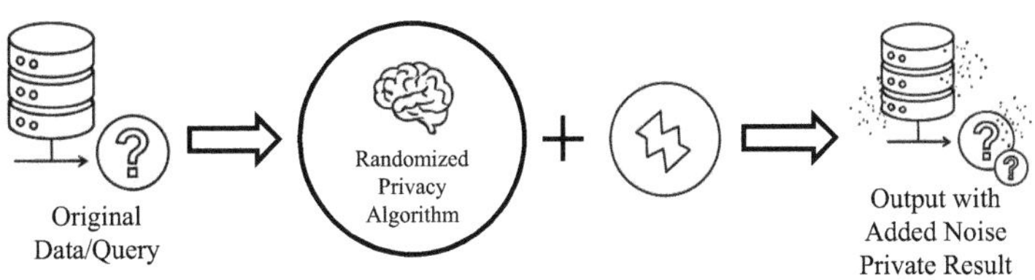

Fig. 2.2 Schematic of the DP mechanism (noise addition process)

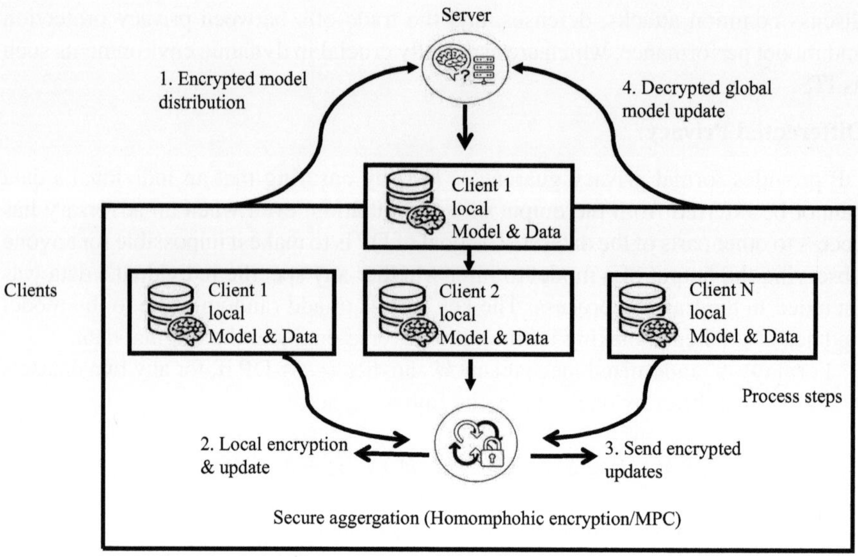

Fig. 2.3 Communication flow of the SecAgg protocol

Secure Aggregation:

SecAgg is a cryptographic protocol [11] designed to protect the privacy of model updates during aggregation in FL (Fig. 2.3). In a typical FL setup, the global model update at round t is expressed as:

$$\mathbf{w}^{t+1} = \sum_{i=1}^{N} \frac{n_i}{n_{\text{total}}} \mathbf{w}_i^t \tag{2.11}$$

where n_i denotes the data size at client i.

However, if the server directly accesses each $\mathbf{w}_i^t$, it may infer client-level data patterns. To prevent this, each client applies encryption $E_i(\cdot)$ before transmission:

$$\mathbf{c}_i^t = E_i(\mathbf{w}_i^t) \tag{2.12}$$

and the server performs aggregation over ciphertexts:

$$\mathbf{C}^t = \sum_{i=1}^{N} \mathbf{c}_i^t \tag{2.13}$$

Since the encryption scheme supports linear operations (e.g., additive homomorphism), the server can compute the global encrypted model $\mathbf{C}^t$ without decrypting individual updates. The aggregated ciphertext is then decrypted jointly by the clients to recover:

$$\mathbf{w}^{t+1} = D(\mathbf{C}^t) \tag{2.14}$$

This guarantees that no single update $\mathbf{w}_i^t$ is visible to the server. Although SecAgg offers strong confidentiality, its computational and communication costs scale with the number of clients N, and encryption operations may introduce latency in large-scale deployments.

Homomorphic Encryption:

HE further strengthens privacy by enabling direct computation on encrypted data. Let $\mathrm{Enc}(\cdot)$ and $\mathrm{Dec}(\cdot)$ denote the encryption and decryption functions. The homomorphic property ensures:

$$\mathrm{Enc}(a) + \mathrm{Enc}(b) = \mathrm{Enc}(a + b), \quad \mathrm{Enc}(a) \times \mathrm{Enc}(b) = \mathrm{Enc}(a \times b) \tag{2.15}$$

Thus, if clients encrypt their local updates $\mathbf{w}_i^t$, the server can compute the global sum:

$$\mathrm{Enc}\left(\mathbf{w}^{t+1}\right) = \sum_{i=1}^{N} \mathrm{Enc}\left(\mathbf{w}_i^t\right) \tag{2.16}$$

and clients can decrypt only after aggregation. HE provides robust privacy but requires high computational overhead, as encryption enlarges the message size and slows operations, which is critical in real-time ITS environments.

Common Attacks and Defenses:

Even with privacy mechanisms, FL remains susceptible to attacks such as:

- **Model Inversion**: adversaries reconstruct private data [18] by exploiting gradients or model outputs.
- **Inference Attacks**: adversaries deduce whether specific samples [49] were used in training.
- **Poisoning Attacks**: malicious clients upload adversarial updates [10] to corrupt the global model.

Defense strategies include:

- **Robust Aggregation**: Using median-based or trimmed mean aggregation [55]:

$$\mathbf{w}^{t+1} = \mathrm{median}\left(\{\mathbf{w}_i^t\}_{i=1}^N\right) \tag{2.17}$$

which reduces the influence of malicious outliers.

- **Gradient Clipping**: Limiting update magnitude [6]:

$$\mathbf{g}_i^t = \frac{\mathbf{g}_i^t}{\max(1, \frac{\|\mathbf{g}_i^t\|_2}{C})} \tag{2.18}$$

where C is a clipping threshold.
- **Anomaly Detection**: Statistical screening for unusual update patterns [19], e.g.,

$$z_i^t = \frac{\|\mathbf{w}_i^t - \bar{\mathbf{w}}^t\|_2}{\sigma_t} \tag{2.19}$$

where updates with $z_i^t > \tau$ (a threshold) are considered anomalous.

Privacy and Model Performance Trade-off:

The integration of privacy mechanisms introduces a fundamental trade-off between security and model performance. For example, when using DP, the expected loss function under noise can be expressed as:

$$\mathcal{L}_{DP} = \mathbb{E}_{\mathcal{N}(0,\sigma^2 I)}[\mathcal{L}(\mathbf{w}_i^t + \mathcal{N})] \tag{2.20}$$

which typically increases the variance of gradient estimates, leading to slower convergence. Similarly, the time complexity of HE and SecAgg-based aggregation [16] grows as:

$$T_{\text{Sec}} = O(N \cdot k + N^2), \quad T_{\text{HE}} = O(N \cdot \text{Enc\_Ops}) \tag{2.21}$$

where k is the key length and Enc_Ops denotes encryption operations per client. Balancing privacy, accuracy, and latency remains an optimization problem for system designers.

Security Needs in ITS:

In ITS, FL must consider additional complexities such as high mobility, heterogeneous devices, and time-sensitive decisions. The privacy and security requirements can be represented as a multi-objective constraint optimization:

$$\min_{\mathbf{w}} \ \mathcal{L}(\mathbf{w}) \quad \text{s.t.} \quad \epsilon \leq \epsilon_{\text{max}}, \ T_{\text{comm}} \leq T_{\text{limit}}, \ \text{Acc}(\mathbf{w}) \geq \alpha_{\text{min}} \tag{2.22}$$

where ϵ_{max} is the maximum privacy budget allowed, T_{comm} is the communication latency constraint, and α_{min} is the minimum accuracy target.

ITS applications such as vehicle-to-vehicle (V2V) or vehicle-to-infrastructure (V2I) networks must maintain real-time responsiveness while safeguarding sensitive driving data and ensuring model integrity under dynamic network conditions. This requires adaptive privacy budgets, lightweight encryption [28], and efficient SecAgg protocols to preserve both safety and learning performance.

2.5 IoT and Edge Computing Infrastructures for Mobility

ITS rely on the integration of IoT devices, edge computing, fog computing, and cloud computing to enable real-time, efficient, and secure mobility solutions. The IoT infrastructure for mobility is typically organized into three primary layers: the perception layer, network layer, and application layer [37]. These layers collectively handle data collection, communication, and decision-making processes, allowing the system to function efficiently. The collaboration of edge, fog, and cloud computing ensures the smooth flow of information and computation between local devices, intermediate nodes, and centralized systems, making it feasible to process and analyze data in real time within an ITS environment (Fig. 2.4).

Mathematical Representation of Layered Data Flow. We can model the flow of information across these three layers as a hierarchical data transmission and computation process [14]. Suppose the data generated by sensor s_i at time t is denoted as $x_i(t)$. The aggregated data received at the fog node f_j can be expressed as:

$$X_{f_j}(t) = \sum_{i \in S_j} \omega_i x_i(t), \tag{2.23}$$

where S_j represents the set of sensors connected to fog node f_j, and ω_i denotes the transmission weight, typically reflecting communication reliability [34] or signal

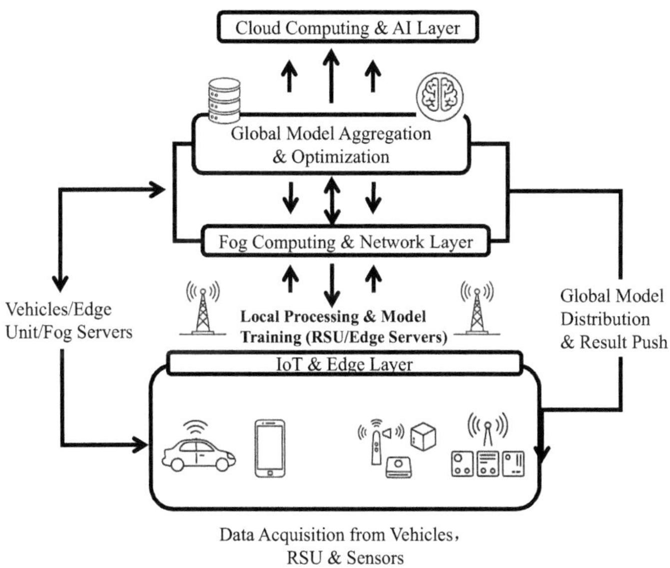

Fig. 2.4 The three-layer IoT–edge–cloud architecture for ITS

strength. This aggregation ensures that only relevant, high-quality data are propagated to the higher layers (fog and cloud), reducing bandwidth usage and ensuring scalability.

In an ITS, the perception layer is the foundation, responsible for collecting data [23] from a wide variety of sensors embedded in vehicles, road infrastructure, and other mobility components. These sensors include cameras, radar, GPS, and environmental monitoring devices that collect data such as traffic flow, vehicle speed, and road conditions. This data is essential for making informed decisions about traffic management, vehicle safety, and AD.

The network layer plays a vital role in transmitting the data gathered by the perception layer to intermediate nodes for processing. It is also responsible for ensuring the efficient and reliable communication between devices, vehicles, and central systems. Communication protocols such as V2X [37], 5G, and Wi-Fi are commonly used in this layer to handle large amounts of data with low latency and high bandwidth. The network layer ensures that the data can flow seamlessly to the correct destinations for analysis or decision-making.

Communication Delay Model. The total communication latency τ_{comm} [17] between the perception and cloud layers can be modeled as:

$$\tau_{comm} = \tau_{uplink} + \tau_{fog} + \tau_{downlink}, \tag{2.24}$$

where τ_{uplink} denotes the data transmission delay from perception devices to fog nodes, τ_{fog} represents the intermediate processing delay at fog nodes, and $\tau_{downlink}$ accounts for the feedback time from the cloud to the edge devices. In latency-sensitive ITS applications, τ_{comm} must satisfy the condition $\tau_{comm} \leq \tau_{max}$, where τ_{max} is the maximum allowable delay for real-time operations such as collision avoidance or adaptive signal control.

At the application layer, the data is processed and utilized for specific tasks, including vehicle safety monitoring, traffic optimization, and autonomous navigation. ML models, such as those used in FL [57], are employed at this layer to leverage the data for real-time predictions and decision-making that can improve traffic flow, reduce congestion, and enhance safety. This layer interacts directly with local devices, enabling real-time control and decision-making for applications like smart traffic lights and AD systems.

The collaboration between edge computing, fog computing, and cloud computing forms the backbone of this infrastructure, providing an efficient system for managing and processing the vast amounts of data generated by IoT devices in the transportation network. Edge computing brings computation closer to the source of data generation—often to the vehicle or RSU—enabling low-latency, real-time decision-making. In autonomous vehicles, for example, edge devices process data from cameras and sensors to make immediate driving decisions. In ITS, edge computing reduces the dependency on centralized systems, helping to mitigate communication delays and enhancing the responsiveness of critical applications.

Computation Distribution Model. Let the total computation task be represented by $\mathcal{T}$, which is distributed among edge, fog, and cloud layers. If the computational capacity of each layer is C_e, C_f, and C_c respectively, then the fraction of task allocated to each layer can be expressed as:

$$\mathcal{T} = \alpha_e C_e + \alpha_f C_f + \alpha_c C_c, \quad \text{where } \alpha_e + \alpha_f + \alpha_c = 1. \tag{2.25}$$

Here, α_e, α_f, and α_c denote the proportion of computation assigned to the edge, fog, and cloud layers, respectively. Optimizing these coefficients ensures minimal latency while maintaining energy efficiency.

Fog computing, situated between edge devices and the cloud [51], provides a layer of processing and storage at intermediate nodes like RSUs or local gateways. This ensures that the data from vehicles and infrastructure does not need to be immediately sent to the cloud for processing, thereby reducing bandwidth requirements and enhancing system efficiency. Fog nodes process and filter the data before transmitting it further, allowing local devices to respond quickly to immediate needs, such as adjusting traffic signals based on vehicle flow or enabling V2V communications. Fog computing acts as a bridge, enhancing data transmission between edge devices and cloud servers, and enabling real-time analytics for transportation systems.

The cloud computing layer is the most centralized component [7] of the system, responsible for long-term data storage, large-scale ML model training, and high-level analytics. Cloud servers handle the aggregation of data from edge and fog layers, enabling the training of global ML models, including FL models, and providing centralized processing resources that support real-time decision-making. The cloud infrastructure also hosts the systems that deliver insights and predictions back to local edge devices, which can then use these models to make decisions in real time.

Federated Model Aggregation Process. When multiple edge devices participate in FL, the cloud aggregates local model updates [25] according to:

$$w_{t+1} = \sum_{k=1}^{K} \frac{n_k}{N} w_t^{(k)}, \tag{2.26}$$

where $w_t^{(k)}$ represents the local model weights from device k at iteration t, n_k is the number of local samples, and $N = \sum_k n_k$ is the total data volume across all devices. This weighted aggregation preserves fairness among devices with heterogeneous data volumes while maintaining model convergence stability.

FL plays a key role in enabling the decentralized model training needed for ITS. In FL, the model training process is distributed across multiple devices, allowing local data from vehicles and infrastructure to be used to train a global model without the need to centralize sensitive data. Data collection occurs at the perception layer, where sensors on vehicles and road-side infrastructure gather data. This data is then processed locally at edge devices, where initial model training takes place. The edge devices send their model updates—rather than raw data—back to the cloud or centralized servers, where they are aggregated to update the global model. This approach maintains the privacy of individual data points while allowing the system to learn from the collective data of all participants. Once the global model is updated in the cloud, it is sent back to the edge devices for deployment, where it is used to make real-time decisions.

In this architecture, edge computing is essential for the success of FL in mobility systems, enabling real-time data processing, local model training, and low-latency decision-making. Edge devices, such as those in vehicles or traffic sensors, play a key role in collecting and processing data locally, which helps minimize latency and ensures that decisions can be made quickly. Fog computing supports the edge layer by processing data from multiple edge devices, filtering and aggregating it to reduce the amount of information that needs to be sent to the cloud. This enables a more scalable and efficient system that can handle the increasing volume of data generated by IoT devices in the transportation network.

As data is processed at the edge and fog layers, it is transmitted to the cloud for further analysis and model updates. The cloud infrastructure, with its centralized processing capabilities, plays a key role in aggregating the model updates from edge and fog nodes to update the global model. The cloud-based servers are also responsible for training more complex ML models that require larger-scale data processing and storage.

The system design also needs to address the challenges posed by data heterogeneity in IoT environments [59]. The data collected by different sensors in ITS can vary widely in format, frequency, and quality. This makes it challenging to design FL architectures that can effectively handle the diversity of data while ensuring that the system remains efficient and scalable. In particular, models must be able to adapt to different types of data, such as video streams from cameras, sensor readings from GPS units, or data from traffic flow sensors, all of which may have different structures and characteristics.

Heterogeneous Data Representation. To represent the diversity of multimodal IoT data [8], we define a unified data descriptor:

$$\mathbf{X} = \{x^{(v)}, x^{(s)}, x^{(g)}\}, \tag{2.27}$$

where $x^{(v)}$ denotes visual data (e.g., camera images), $x^{(s)}$ represents sensor readings (e.g., speed or acceleration), and $x^{(g)}$ denotes geolocation data from GPS. Each modality can have distinct sampling rates and feature dimensions, making feature alignment and model fusion crucial for effective FL.

Real-time processing and low-latency requirements [9, 27] are also significant challenges for FL in mobility systems. Edge computing plays a crucial role in ensuring that decisions can be made quickly, especially in time-sensitive applications such as autonomous vehicle navigation and dynamic traffic management. The cloud, while crucial for model aggregation and long-term insights, cannot always be relied upon for real-time decision-making due to communication delays and bandwidth constraints.

In conclusion, edge computing is the cornerstone of FL in ITS, enabling real-time data processing and decision-making. The integration of edge, fog, and cloud computing creates a robust infrastructure [3] that supports large-scale, privacy-preserving ML while reducing latency and computational load. However, challenges related to data heterogeneity and real-time processing must be addressed to optimize the system's performance and scalability. The successful deployment of FL in mobility systems requires a careful balance between local processing capabilities, real-time decision-making, and centralized model aggregation to ensure efficient and secure operation in dynamic, data-rich environments.

2.6 Integration of FL and IoT

The integration of FL with the IoT in ITS presents both tremendous opportunities and complex challenges. As the number of connected devices in transportation networks grows, it is increasingly important to address issues such as energy efficiency, communication bandwidth, and the allocation of computational resources. In particular, FL needs to be optimized to work effectively within the resource-constrained environment of IoT [33, 38], where devices like sensors and vehicles often face limitations in power, bandwidth, and processing capacity.

A critical challenge in integrating FL with IoT lies in the efficient distribution of computation and communication tasks. In IoT-enabled ITS, devices generate vast amounts of data that need to be processed and shared. However, these devices are often constrained by limited energy resources, which makes it difficult to carry out extensive computations or maintain continuous communication with central servers. FL exacerbates these constraints because it requires frequent model updates from edge devices to the cloud for global aggregation. These frequent transmissions and computations can place a heavy burden on the energy budgets of IoT devices, leading to the need for sophisticated energy-aware resource allocation strategies.

The total energy consumption $\mathcal{E}_i$ of an IoT device i during one training round can be expressed as:

$$\mathcal{E}_i = \mathcal{E}_i^{comp} + \mathcal{E}_i^{comm}, \tag{2.28}$$

where $\mathcal{E}_i^{comp}$ denotes the computation energy for local training [52], and $\mathcal{E}_i^{comm}$ represents the energy consumed during communication with the edge or cloud server. For local computation, the energy consumption is given by:

$$\mathcal{E}_i^{comp} = \kappa_i C_i D_i f_i^2, \tag{2.29}$$

where κ_i is the effective capacitance coefficient, C_i is the number of CPU cycles required per data sample, D_i is the local data size, and f_i is the CPU frequency. This quadratic dependence on f_i indicates that higher computation speed comes at the cost of increased power consumption.

For communication, the transmission energy can be modeled [5] as:

$$\mathcal{E}_i^{comm} = p_i^{tx} \cdot \frac{s_i}{R_i}, \tag{2.30}$$

where p_i^{tx} is the transmission power, s_i is the model update size in bits, and R_i is the uplink transmission rate. The transmission rate is determined by Shannon's capacity formula:

$$R_i = B_i \log_2 \left(1 + \frac{p_i^{tx} h_i}{N_0}\right), \tag{2.31}$$

where B_i is the allocated bandwidth, h_i denotes the channel gain, and N_0 is the noise power spectral density. This formulation shows how communication efficiency is bounded by both physical and network-level parameters.

To address these challenges, one potential solution is the use of edge computing, which offloads computational tasks from IoT devices to nearby edge nodes like RSUs or local gateways. These edge devices have more computational resources and can perform more intensive processing tasks, such as aggregating model updates and conducting local training. By using edge-assisted FL, IoT devices can perform lighter computations locally and send only aggregated updates to the edge, thereby reducing the amount of data transmitted and conserving energy.

Moreover, communication bandwidth is another pressing issue in the integration of FL with IoT. In ITS, communication between devices and central systems can be limited by bandwidth constraints [25], particularly in high-density environments where many devices generate continuous streams of data. This issue becomes more acute in FL, as each device needs to transmit its local model updates periodically. If these updates are large or frequent, network congestion and high latency can result, degrading the system's overall performance.

The communication delay τ_i [35] for device i can be represented as:

$$\tau_i = \frac{s_i}{R_i}, \tag{2.32}$$

and the total system latency τ_{total} across N devices in one round of FL training is:

$$\tau_{total} = \max_{i \in \mathcal{N}} \left(\tau_i^{comp} + \tau_i^{comm}\right), \tag{2.33}$$

where τ_i^{comp} and τ_i^{comm} denote the local computation and communication time, respectively. Reducing τ_{total} is critical for real-time ITS applications, as it directly influences the system responsiveness for tasks such as vehicle coordination or congestion control.

Efficient communication strategies are therefore essential to ensuring that FL operates smoothly in ITS environments. One potential solution is to employ advanced task scheduling algorithms that prioritize important updates and aggregate smaller updates before transmission, reducing the communication overhead.

The integration of FL with IoT in ITS requires a multi-layer aggregation approach, where model updates are aggregated at different levels: device, edge, and cloud. At the device level, local IoT devices, such as sensors in vehicles or infrastructure, collect data and train local models based on their observations. These models are then updated and sent to edge devices for further aggregation.

The hierarchical aggregation process [1] can be mathematically represented as:

$$w^{(t+1)} = \sum_{e \in \mathcal{E}} \lambda_e \left(\sum_{i \in C_e} \lambda_i w_i^{(t)} \right), \tag{2.34}$$

where $\mathcal{E}$ denotes the set of edge nodes, C_e represents the set of IoT devices under edge node e, λ_i and λ_e are local and edge-level aggregation weights, respectively, and $w_i^{(t)}$ is the local model from device i at iteration t. This hierarchical aggregation ensures distributed computation, reduces network load, and achieves scalable model convergence.

In terms of specific models for integrating FL with IoT, several approaches have been proposed. One common model is edge-assisted FL [39], where edge devices perform the heavy lifting in terms of computation and aggregation, allowing IoT devices to focus on data collection and light model updates (Fig. 2.5).

Another model is clustered FL, where IoT devices are grouped into clusters based on factors such as geographical proximity or data similarity. Each cluster trains its own local model, and only aggregated updates from each cluster are sent to the cloud. The local cluster update process can be expressed as:

$$w_c^{(t+1)} = \sum_{i \in C_c} \lambda_i w_i^{(t)}, \tag{2.35}$$

where $w_c^{(t+1)}$ represents the aggregated model of cluster c. This approach reduces communication overhead and enhances scalability for large-scale ITS applications.

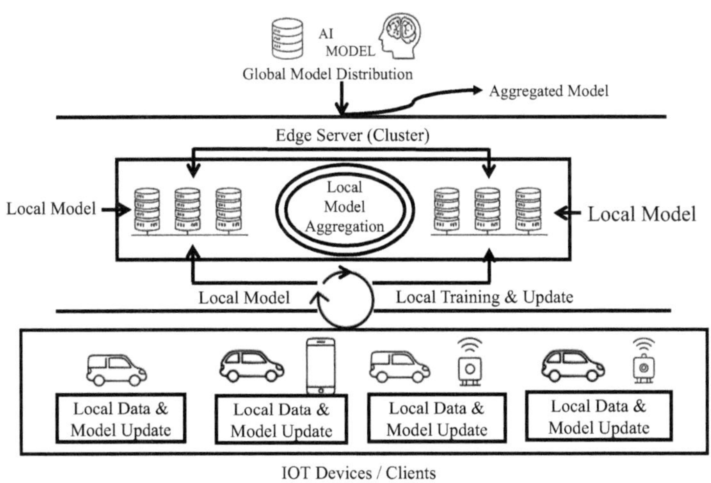

Fig. 2.5 Framework for edge-assisted FL in an IoT environment

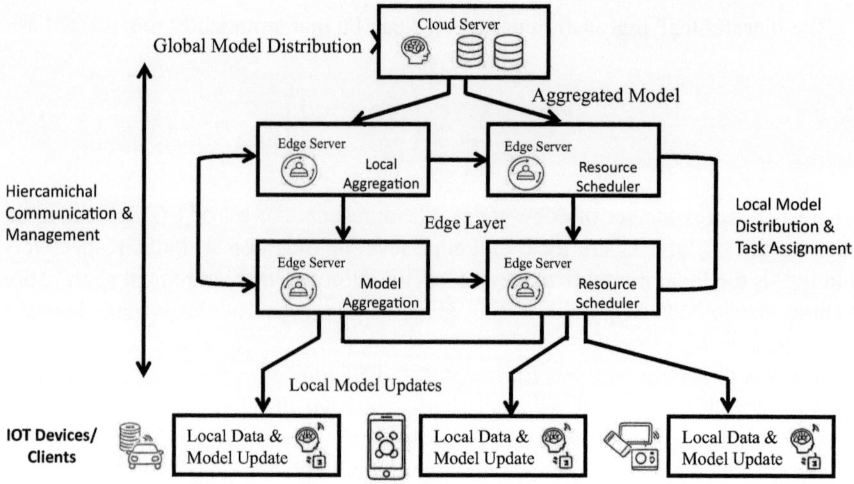

Fig. 2.6 Schematic of hierarchical aggregation and resource scheduling in an FL-IoT system

A third model is hierarchical FL (Fig. 2.6), which introduces multiple levels of aggregation. In this model, updates from local devices are aggregated at the edge layer and then sent to the cloud for further aggregation. This hierarchical structure ensures that model updates are efficiently handled at the local level, while still enabling global aggregation at the cloud level. Hierarchical FL offers scalability and flexibility, especially in large and heterogeneous ITS environments where devices vary in terms of computational power and communication capabilities.

The integration of FL with IoT also requires careful consideration of delay and energy consumption. In ITS, minimizing delay is crucial, particularly for applications like AD and traffic management, where real-time decision-making is needed. The end-to-end response time τ_{end} can be expressed as:

$$\tau_{end} = \tau_i^{comp} + \tau_i^{comm} + \tau_{agg}, \tag{2.36}$$

where τ_{agg} is the aggregation delay at edge or cloud servers. This value reflects the total latency from data collection to model deployment.

To address these concerns, dynamic resource scheduling is essential. Resource scheduling aims to optimize the trade-off between energy consumption and latency, which can be formulated as:

$$\min_{S} \alpha \sum_i \mathcal{E}_i + \beta \tau_{total}, \tag{2.37}$$

subject to device resource constraints, where α and β are weighting factors balancing energy and delay objectives, and S represents the scheduling strategy. This optimization ensures efficient energy usage and timely model convergence across heterogeneous IoT devices.

Finally, the concept of Green FL emerges as a promising solution for minimizing the environmental impact of IoT and FL systems. Green FL focuses on reducing energy consumption and carbon emissions by optimizing the energy use of edge devices and cloud infrastructures. The carbon footprint C_{total} of the system can be represented as:

$$C_{total} = \eta_{cloud}\mathcal{E}_{cloud} + \sum_{e\in\mathcal{E}} \eta_e \mathcal{E}_e + \sum_{i\in\mathcal{N}} \eta_i \mathcal{E}_i, \tag{2.38}$$

where η_{cloud}, η_e, and η_i are emission coefficients corresponding to cloud, edge, and device layers, respectively. By incorporating sustainability principles into the design of FL systems, ITS can move toward greener and more efficient solutions for smart mobility.

In conclusion, the integration of FL with IoT in ITS holds great promise for enhancing scalability, efficiency, and privacy. However, challenges related to energy efficiency, communication bandwidth, and multi-layer aggregation must be addressed to optimize the performance of these systems. Models such as edge-assisted FL, clustered FL, and hierarchical FL provide flexible solutions that balance computational power, communication efficiency, and real-time performance. By integrating dynamic resource scheduling and green FL strategies, ITS can move toward a more sustainable, adaptive, and efficient federated intelligence system.

Summary

This chapter provided an in-depth exploration of the key technologies and strategies integral to the deployment of FL in ITS. We began by establishing the architectural foundation required for successful FL implementation in ITS, emphasizing the layered approach involving the perception, network, and application layers. These layers provide the necessary infrastructure for data collection, communication, and real-time processing, forming the backbone of an IoT-enabled smart mobility system.

Next, we delved into the core algorithms driving FL, including FedAvg, FedProx, and FedOpt, highlighting their roles in distributed model training. These algorithms facilitate efficient learning without the need to centralize sensitive data, addressing the challenges posed by communication overhead and system heterogeneity. In parallel, we discussed privacy and security mechanisms essential for protecting the integrity of the system, including DP, SecAgg, and HE. These techniques ensure that user data remains secure while still enabling the aggregation of model updates across a distributed network.

We also explored the integration of IoT with edge, fog, and cloud computing infrastructures, outlining the importance of efficient resource management and the need for multi-level aggregation. The IoT devices at the edge collect data, which is processed at local, intermediate, and cloud-based levels, ensuring that model updates are handled in an optimized manner, minimizing latency and energy consumption. The chapter further addressed key challenges such as energy efficiency, communication bandwidth, and dynamic resource allocation, presenting solutions like edge-assisted FL and hierarchical FL to overcome these limitations.

The fusion of FL and IoT was examined in detail, with a focus on how different FL models, such as edge-assisted, clustered, and hierarchical FL, can be employed to address the unique demands of ITS. We also discussed how dynamic scheduling and green FL strategies could help balance energy consumption with real-time performance, contributing to the sustainability of ITS applications.

Looking forward, the integration of FL with ITS opens several promising avenues for future research. Emerging technologies like 6G networks and blockchain are poised to play a pivotal role in enhancing the scalability, security, and efficiency of FL systems. Additionally, the combination of edge intelligence and distributed ML will allow for even more efficient and responsive systems, reducing latency and improving real-time decision-making. The exploration of these future technologies will likely propel ITS toward even more intelligent, secure, and sustainable systems, with applications ranging from AD to traffic management and beyond.

These foundational technologies and strategies provide the basis for the next chapter, where we will delve into the practical application of FL in real-world ITS, demonstrating how these concepts can be translated into impactful solutions for smart mobility.

References

1. Abad, M.S.H., Ozfatura, E., Gunduz, D., Ercetin, O.: Hierarchical federated learning across heterogeneous cellular networks. In: ICASSP 2020–2020 IEEE International Conference on Acoustics, Speech and Signal Processing (ICASSP), pp. 8866–8870. IEEE (2020)
2. Abadi, M., Chu, A., Goodfellow, I., McMahan, H.B., Mironov, I., Talwar, K., Zhang, L.: Deep learning with differential privacy. In: Proceedings of the 2016 ACM SIGSAC Conference on Computer and Communications Security, pp. 308–318 (2016)
3. Ai, Y., Peng, M., Zhang, K.: Edge computing technologies for internet of things: a primer. Digital Commun. Netw. **4**(2), 77–86 (2018)
4. Alistarh, D., Grubic, D., Li, J., Tomioka, R., Vojnovic, M.: Qsgd: communication-efficient sgd via gradient quantization and encoding. Adv. Neural Inf. Process. Syst. **30** (2017)
5. Amiri, M.M., Gündüz, D.: Federated learning over wireless fading channels. IEEE Trans. Wirel. Commun. **19**(5), 3546–3557 (2020)
6. Andrew, G., Thakkar, O., McMahan, B., Ramaswamy, S.: Differentially private learning with adaptive clipping. Adv. Neural. Inf. Process. Syst. **34**, 17455–17466 (2021)
7. Armbrust, M., Fox, A., Griffith, R., Joseph, A.D., Katz, R., Konwinski, A., Lee, G., Patterson, D., Rabkin, A., Stoica, I., et al.: A view of cloud computing. Commun. ACM **53**(4), 50–58 (2010)
8. Atrey, P.K., Hossain, M.A., El Saddik, A., Kankanhalli, M.S.: Multimodal fusion for multimedia analysis: a survey. Multimedia Syst. **16**(6), 345–379 (2010)
9. Babar, M., Arif, F.: Real-time data processing scheme using big data analytics in internet of things based smart transportation environment. J. Ambient. Intell. Humaniz. Comput. **10**(10), 4167–4177 (2019)
10. Bhagoji, A.N., Chakraborty, S., Mittal, P., Calo, S.: Analyzing federated learning through an adversarial lens. In: International Conference on Machine Learning, PMLR, pp. 634–64 (2019)

11. Bonawitz, K., Ivanov, V., Kreuter, B., Marcedone, A., McMahan, H.B., Patel, S., Ramage, D., Segal, A., Seth, K.: Practical secure aggregation for privacy-preserving machine learning. In: Proceedings of the 2017 ACM SIGSAC Conference on Computer and Communications Security, pp. 1175–1191 (2017)
12. Chellapandi, V.P., Yuan, L., Brinton, C.G., Zak, S.H., Wang, Z.: Federated learning for connected and automated vehicles: a survey of existing approaches and challenges. IEEE Trans. Intell. Veh. **9**(1), 119–137 (2023)
13. Cho, Y.J., Wang, J., Joshi, G.: Client selection in federated learning: convergence analysis and power-of-choice selection strategies (2020). arXiv:2010.01243
14. Din, S., Paul, A., Rehman, A.: 5g-enabled hierarchical architecture for software-defined intelligent transportation system. Comput. Netw. **150**, 81–89 (2019)
15. Dwork, C., McSherry, F., Nissim, K., Smith, A.: Calibrating noise to sensitivity in private data analysis. In: Theory of Cryptography Conference, pp. 265–284. Springer, Berlin (2006)
16. Elhattab, F.: Robust and privacy-preserving federated learning. Ph.D. thesis, INSA de Lyon (2023)
17. Fan, Q., Bai, J., Zhang, H., Yi, Y., Liu, L.: Delay-aware resource allocation in fog-assisted IoT networks through reinforcement learning. IEEE Internet Things J. **9**(7), 5189–5199 (2021)
18. Fredrikson, M., Jha, S., Ristenpart, T.: Model inversion attacks that exploit confidence information and basic countermeasures. In: Proceedings of the 22nd ACM SIGSAC Conference on Computer and Communications Security, pp. 1322–1333 (2015)
19. Fung, C., Yoon, C.J., Beschastnikh, I.: The limitations of federated learning in sybil settings. In: 23rd International Symposium on Research in Attacks, Intrusions and Defenses (RAID 2020), pp. 301–316 (2020)
20. Geyer, R.C., Klein, T., Nabi, M.: Differentially Private Federated Learning: A Client Level Perspective (2017). arXiv:1712.07557
21. Goetz, J., Malik, K., Bui, D., Moon, S., Liu, H., Kumar, A.: Active federated learning (2019). arXiv:1909.12641
22. Karimireddy, S.P., Kale, S., Mohri, M., Reddi, S., Stich, S., Suresh, A.T.: Scaffold: stochastic controlled averaging for federated learning. In: International Conference on Machine Learning, pp. 5132–5143, PMLR (2020)
23. Kashinath, S.A., Mostafa, S.A., Mustapha, A., Mahdin, H., Lim, D., Mahmoud, M.A., Mohammed, M.A., Al-Rimy, B.A.S., Fudzee, M.F.M., Yang, T.J.: Review of data fusion methods for real-time and multi-sensor traffic flow analysis. IEEE Access **9**, 51258–51276 (2021)
24. Khan, L.U., Mustafa, E., Shuja, J., Rehman, F., Bilal, K., Han, Z., Hong, C.S.: Federated learning for digital twin-based vehicular networks: architecture and challenges. IEEE Wirel. Commun. **31**(2), 156–162 (2023)
25. Konečnỳ, J., McMahan, H.B., Yu, F.X., Richtárik, P., Suresh, A.T., Bacon, D.: Federated learning: strategies for improving communication efficiency (2016). arXiv:1610.05492
26. Lalitha, A., Shekhar, S., Javidi, T., Koushanfar, F.: Fully decentralized federated learning. In: Third Workshop on Bayesian Deep Learning (NeurIPS), vol. 12 (2018)
27. Li, H., Shou, G., Hu, Y., Guo, Z.: Mobile edge computing: progress and challenges. In: 2016 4th IEEE International Conference on Mobile Cloud Computing, Services, and Engineering (MobileCloud), pp. 83–84. IEEE (2016)
28. Li, Q., Wang, W., Zhu, Y., Ying, Z.: Boppcl: blockchain-enabled opportunistic federated learning applied in intelligent transportation systems. Electronics **13**(1), 136 (2023)
29. Li, T., Sahu, A.K., Zaheer, M., Sanjabi, M., Talwalkar, A., Smith, V.: Federated optimization in heterogeneous networks. Proc. Mach. Learn. Syst. **2**, 429–450 (2020)
30. Li, X., Huang, K., Yang, W., Wang, S., Zhang, Z.: On the convergence of fedavg on non-iid data (2019a). arXiv:1907.02189
31. Li, Y., Yang, S., Ren, X., Zhao, C.: Asynchronous federated learning with differential privacy for edge intelligence (2019b). arXiv:1912.07902
32. Liang, X., Liu, Y., Chen, T., Liu, M., Yang, Q.: Federated transfer reinforcement learning for autonomous driving. In: Federated and Transfer Learning, pp. 357–371. Springer, Berlin (2022)

33. Lim, W.Y.B., Luong, N.C., Hoang, D.T., Jiao, Y., Liang, Y.C., Yang, Q., Niyato, D., Miao, C.: Federated learning in mobile edge networks: a comprehensive survey. IEEE Commun. Surv. Tutorials **22**(3), 2031–2063 (2020)
34. Liu, L., Chen, C., Pei, Q., Maharjan, S., Zhang, Y.: Vehicular edge computing and networking: a survey. Mobile Netw. Appl. **26**(3), 1145–1168 (2021)
35. Luo, B., Li, X., Wang, S., Huang, J., Tassiulas, L.: Cost-effective federated learning in mobile edge networks. IEEE J. Sel. Areas Commun. **39**(12), 3606–3621 (2021)
36. Mothukuri, V., Parizi, R.M., Pouriyeh, S., Huang, Y., Dehghantanha, A., Srivastava, G.: A survey on security and privacy of federated learning. Future Gener. Comput. Syst. **115**, 619–640 (2021)
37. Muthuramalingam, S., Bharathi, A., Rakesh Kumar, S., Gayathri, N., Sathiyaraj, R., Balamurugan, B.: IoT based intelligent transportation system (IoT-its) for global perspective: a case study. In: Internet of Things and Big Data Analytics for Smart Generation, pp. 279–300. Springer, Berlin (2018)
38. Nguyen, D.C., Ding, M., Pathirana, P.N., Seneviratne, A., Li, J., Poor, H.V.: Federated learning for internet of things: a comprehensive survey. IEEE Commun. Surv. Tutorials **23**(3), 1622–1658 (2021)
39. Nishio, T., Yonetani, R.: Client selection for federated learning with heterogeneous resources in mobile edge. In: ICC 2019–2019 IEEE International Conference on Communications (ICC), pp. 1–7. IEEE (2019)
40. Pei, J.: F3: fair federated learning framework with adaptive regularization. Knowl.-Based Syst. **316**, 113392 (2025)
41. Pei, J., Yu, Z., Liu, W., Kong, W., Zhang, J., Wang, L.: Clustered federated learning multi-classifier for non-iid scenario in drone devices. In: Proceedings of the 5th International ACM Mobicom Workshop on Drone Assisted Wireless Communications for 5G and Beyond, pp. 79–84 (2022)
42. Pei, J., Zhong, K., Li, J., Yu, Z.: Pac: partial area clustering for re-adjusting the layout of traffic stations in city's public transport. IEEE Trans. Intell. Transp. Syst. **24**(1), 1251–1260 (2022)
43. Pei, J., Liu, W., Wang, L., Liu, C., Bashir, A.K., Wang, Y.: Fed-iout: opportunities and challenges of federated learning in the internet of underwater things. IEEE Internet Things Mag. **6**(1), 108–112 (2023)
44. Pei, J., Li, W., Mumtaz, S.: From routine to reflection: pruning neural networks in communication-efficient federated learning. IEEE Trans. Artif. Intell. (2024)
45. Pei, J., Dai, M., Prasad, R.V., Alghamdi, N.S., Al-Otaibi, Y.D., Bashir, A.K.: Fl meets llm: a hybrid security framework for the internet of energy. IEEE Netw. (2025b)
46. Pei, J., Li, J., Song, Z., Al Dabel, M.M., Alenazi, M.J., Zhang, S., Bashir, A.K.: Neuro-vae-symbolic dynamic traffic management. IEEE Trans. Intell. Transp. Syst. (2025b)
47. Posner, J., Tseng, L., Aloqaily, M., Jararweh, Y.: Federated learning in vehicular networks: opportunities and solutions. IEEE Netw. **35**(2), 152–159 (2021)
48. Reddi, S., Charles, Z., Zaheer, M., Garrett, Z., Rush, K., Konečnỳ, J., Kumar, S., McMahan, H.B.: Adaptive federated optimization (2020). arXiv:2003.00295
49. Shokri, R., Stronati, M., Song, C., Shmatikov, V.: Membership inference attacks against machine learning models. In: 2017 IEEE Symposium on Security and Privacy (SP), pp. 3–18. IEEE (2017)
50. Sun, H., Pei, J., Xu, X., Xue, R., Zhao, L., Sun, Q., Li, L., Wang, L.: Fedmkd: multi-teacher knowledge distillation for communication-efficient federated learning. Clust. Comput. **28**(10), 638 (2025)
51. Vaquero, L.M., Rodero-Merino, L.: Finding your way in the fog: towards a comprehensive definition of fog computing. ACM SIGCOMM Comput. Commun. Rev. **44**(5), 27–32 (2014)
52. Wang, J., Liu, Q., Liang, H., Joshi, G., Poor, H.V.: Tackling the objective inconsistency problem in heterogeneous federated optimization. Adv. Neural. Inf. Process. Syst. **33**, 7611–7623 (2020)
53. Xia, H., Xu, S., Pei, J., Zhang, R., Yu, Z., Zou, W., Wang, L., Liu, C.: Fedme 2: memory evaluation and erase promoting federated unlearning in dtmn. IEEE J. Sel. Areas Commun. **41**(11), 3573–3588 (2023)

54. Xu, R., Baracaldo, N., Zhou, Y., Anwar, A., Joshi, J., Ludwig, H.: Fedv: Privacy-preserving federated learning over vertically partitioned data. In: Proceedings of the 14th ACM Workshop on Artificial Intelligence and Security, pp. 181–192 (2021)
55. Yin, D., Chen, Y., Kannan, R., Bartlett, P.: Byzantine-robust distributed learning: Towards optimal statistical rates. In: International Conference on Machine Learning, pp. 5650–5659. PMLR (2018)
56. Yu, Z., Huang, Z., Pei, J., Tahsin, L., Sun, D.: Semantic-oriented feature coupling transformer for vehicle re-identification in intelligent transportation system. IEEE Trans. Intell. Transp. Syst. **25**(3), 2803–2813 (2023)
57. Zhang, R., Mao, J., Wang, H., Li, B., Cheng, X., Yang, L.: A survey on federated learning in intelligent transportation systems. IEEE Trans. Intell. Veh. (2024)
58. Zhang, X., Yin, W., Hong, M., Chen, T.: Hybrid federated learning: algorithms and implementation (2020). arXiv:2012.12420
59. Zhao, Y., Li, M., Lai, L., Suda, N., Civin, D., Chandra, V.: Federated learning with non-iid data (2018). arXiv:1806.00582

Chapter 3
FL Applications in Smart Mobility

Abstract Building upon the foundational concepts of FL introduced in Chap. 2, this chapter delves into the diverse applications of FL in smart mobility systems. We explore how FL can enhance AD, particularly in cooperative perception between vehicles to improve safety and navigation. Additionally, the role of FL in TFP and intelligent signal control is examined, highlighting its potential for real-time, data-driven traffic management. We also investigate how FL optimizes personalized mobility services, such as adaptive route recommendations, and addresses security concerns in V2X communication. Furthermore, the potential of FL to support sustainable and energy-efficient mobility solutions is discussed. The chapter concludes with a summary of key insights and future directions for FL in the transportation sector.

Keywords FL · AD · TFP · Personalized mobility · V2X · Connected vehicles · Energy efficiency · Smart mobility · Sustainability

3.1 AD and Cooperative Perception

AD represents a breakthrough in transportation, promising enhanced safety, convenience, and efficiency. At the core of AD systems is the perception framework [7, 59], which enables vehicles to detect [11, 43] and understand their environment in real time. However, the development of effective AD systems hinges on addressing several challenges in perception systems, including the integration of multi-source data, ensuring real-time responsiveness, and maintaining safety in dynamic environments.

The perception system of an autonomous vehicle relies on a variety of sensors [17], such as cameras, LiDAR, radar, and ultrasonic sensors, which capture different types of data. These diverse data streams must be processed to create an accurate and reliable model of the vehicle's surroundings. This involves tasks such as object detection, road boundary identification, and the tracking of surrounding vehicles. The central challenge arises from the multi-source nature of the data, as each sensor offers unique perspectives but also has inherent limitations. For instance, cameras

© The Author(s), under exclusive license to Springer Nature Singapore Pte Ltd. 2026

J. Pei et al., *Federated Learning for Smart Mobility*, SpringerBriefs in Computer Science,
https://doi.org/10.1007/978-981-95-6160-5_3

are effective for visual object detection but struggle in low-light conditions, while LiDAR provides rich 3D spatial data but is more expensive and less effective in adverse weather conditions like heavy rain or fog.

In real-world driving scenarios, these sensors must operate cohesively to ensure timely and safe decision-making. The need for real-time perception is particularly critical [6, 44, 52] in high-speed driving environments where delayed decisions can lead to dangerous outcomes. Safety remains the primary concern, as any failures in perception—such as missing a pedestrian or misidentifying an obstacle—can lead to catastrophic consequences.

A significant challenge in deploying autonomous vehicles is the issue of data sharing between vehicles [39] and across manufacturers. Autonomous vehicles rely on extensive datasets to train their ML models, but much of this data is proprietary, with differing policies across manufacturers. The challenge, therefore, is to enable collaborative learning while maintaining data privacy and safeguarding competitive advantages.

FL offers a promising solution to this data-sharing challenge. It allows vehicles to collaborate in training ML models without sharing raw data. Instead of transmitting data to a central server for processing, each vehicle trains its model locally using the data it collects, and only model updates—such as gradients or weights—are sent to a central server. The server aggregates these updates to improve the global model, which is then redistributed to the vehicles. This decentralized approach allows vehicles from different manufacturers to contribute to improving perception models while keeping their data private.

In the context of cooperative perception [1] for AD, FL enables vehicles to collaboratively enhance their object detection, semantic segmentation, and sensor fusion models. By training on data collected from various environments, the models benefit from a wider range of experiences, improving their accuracy and robustness. FL ensures that each vehicle can contribute to the learning process while protecting its sensitive data. This collaborative learning approach is particularly valuable in dynamic environments, where the model must adapt to new or rare scenarios, such as unusual road conditions, poor weather, or different traffic patterns.

The architecture of FL in cooperative perception involves multiple layers: local vehicles, edge nodes (such as road-side units or RSUs), and cloud infrastructure (Fig. 3.1). Vehicles serve as local clients, processing data from their sensors to train local models. Edge nodes, typically located at intersections or along highways, act as intermediary aggregation points, collecting model updates from nearby vehicles. The cloud infrastructure then serves as the central hub, where updates from edge devices are aggregated to create a global model. This multi-layered aggregation approach ensures efficient use of computational and communication resources, while enabling real-time model updates as new data becomes available.

Object detection and semantic segmentation are vital components of AD perception systems. Object detection allows [32] the vehicle to identify and classify objects like pedestrians, cyclists, and other vehicles, while semantic segmentation [8] involves classifying each pixel in an image, offering a detailed understanding of

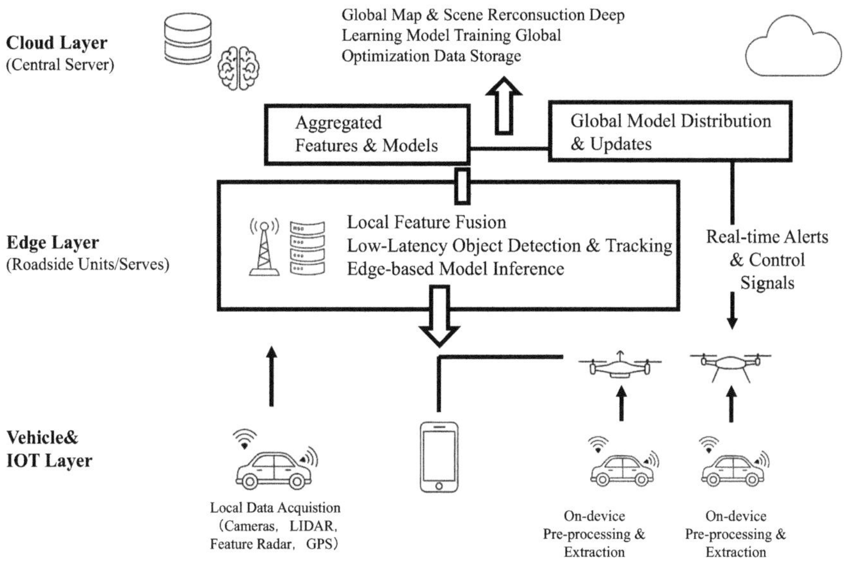

Fig. 3.1 The Vehicle–Edge–Cloud architecture for collaborative perception in AD

the environment. Both tasks rely heavily on accurate and diverse datasets, which can be enhanced through FL.

In object detection, FL allows vehicles to collaboratively improve detection models by exchanging model updates instead of raw data. For instance, a vehicle driving in an urban area might accumulate data rich in pedestrians, while a vehicle in a rural area may encounter more wildlife or livestock. By pooling model updates from these varied environments, a more generalized object detection model can be developed, improving the vehicle's ability to detect a wide range of objects regardless of its operating environment.

Similarly, in semantic segmentation, FL enables vehicles to train models that classify each pixel in an image, which is crucial for understanding road boundaries, lane markings, and obstacles. This task is essential for applications like lane detection, road marking identification, and obstacle avoidance. Given that different environments present unique challenges—such as varying road conditions or different weather patterns—collaborative learning leads to a more generalized and robust model that performs well across diverse conditions.

Moreover, FL facilitates the integration of multiple sensor types (camera, LiDAR, radar) to create a more accurate perception model (Fig. 3.2). Vehicles can share model updates based on the fusion of data from these sensors, improving the accuracy of detection and segmentation tasks while ensuring data privacy.

Data privacy remains a critical concern in AD [50]. Manufacturers may be hesitant to share their raw sensor data with competitors due to proprietary concerns or the potential for misuse. FL mitigates these concerns by ensuring that sensitive data

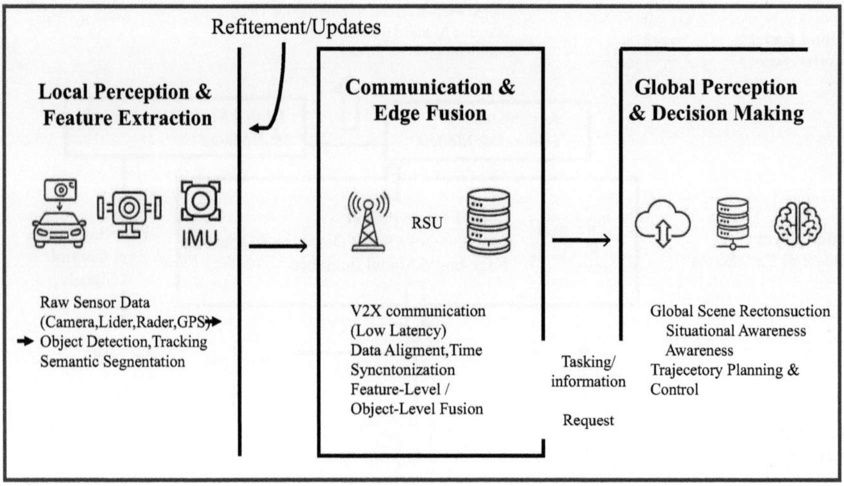

Fig. 3.2 A flowchart illustrating the perception fusion process, integrating data from multiple sensors

never leaves the vehicle. Instead, only model updates, which are less sensitive than raw data, are shared, reducing the risk of data leakage.

Additionally, FL allows vehicles from different manufacturers to collaborate on improving models while maintaining data privacy. For instance, an autonomous vehicle manufacturer may use FL to share updates for object detection models with a fleet of partner vehicles, allowing for cross-manufacturer collaboration. This eliminates the need to transfer raw data, while still enabling the benefits of collaborative learning.

The privacy of FL is further protected by SecAgg techniques [37], which ensure that model updates are combined in a way that prevents any single participant from learning about the updates of others. This makes FL a powerful tool for overcoming the data-sharing barriers that have historically hindered collaboration in the AD domain.

Several companies and research initiatives are exploring FL in AD. For instance, Apollo, Baidu's AD platform [23], has examined the application of FL to enhance object detection models across a fleet of vehicles. By enabling vehicles to share model updates, Apollo aims to create more accurate and generalized models for object detection, improving the safety of its self-driving vehicles.

Tesla, a pioneer in AD [27], uses data from its extensive fleet to train self-driving models. While Tesla has not fully adopted FL, its continuous model updates based on real-world driving data suggest a path toward more collaborative model training. In the future, Tesla could leverage FL to improve cooperation with other manufacturers while maintaining data privacy.

NVIDIA DRIVE, offering a comprehensive platform for AD, has also explored FL to improve object detection and sensor fusion. By using FL, NVIDIA DRIVE enables vehicles to collaborate on model improvements without sharing raw data, combining the benefits of collaborative learning and privacy protection.

Despite these advancements, challenges remain, such as the scalability of FL [24] for large fleets, managing communication overhead, and addressing data heterogeneity. Additionally, further work is needed to ensure that FL operates efficiently in dynamic environments, where models must be frequently updated to accommodate changing conditions.

FL offers a promising solution for collaborative perception in AD, enabling vehicles to learn from each other's experiences while preserving data privacy. By allowing models to be updated collaboratively without the need for raw data sharing, FL enhances the accuracy and reliability of object detection, semantic segmentation, and sensor fusion. Although challenges related to scalability, communication efficiency, and data heterogeneity persist, the integration of FL in AD systems is poised to significantly improve safety, performance, and collaboration across manufacturers. As FL continues to evolve, it will play a key role in shaping the future of autonomous vehicles, enabling them to adapt to diverse environments while maintaining privacy and security.

3.2 TFP and Intelligent Signal Control

TFP is a crucial component in ITS, enabling proactive road network management, reducing congestion, and enhancing safety. However, predicting traffic flow presents several challenges, including data dispersion [35], the temporal and spatial dependencies [20] within the data, and the privacy-sensitive nature of the data [60].

In traffic systems, data is often distributed across various sensors, such as cameras, GPS-enabled vehicles, and mobile devices, located at intersections, highways, and other key points. These sensors collect data in diverse formats and with varying levels of granularity. Aggregating this dispersed data into a unified model is a significant challenge, requiring the handling of inconsistencies, noise, and sparse data from less-covered areas.

Traffic data also exhibits strong temporal and spatial dependencies. The conditions at a particular intersection or road segment are often influenced by previous traffic flow and the traffic conditions at neighboring locations. For instance, congestion on a highway can have downstream effects on traffic flow at exit ramps. Traditional ML methods struggle to model these complex spatiotemporal relationships effectively, especially with large-scale, real-time data streams that need continuous updates.

Furthermore, the privacy sensitivity of traffic data adds another layer of complexity. Raw traffic data often includes sensitive information about individual drivers, such as their location, speed, and travel patterns. Sharing this data raises privacy concerns, particularly when data crosses city or jurisdictional boundaries. Ensuring that data can be shared and processed collaboratively without violating privacy regulations is essential for developing effective TFP systems.

FL offers a promising solution to these challenges [41] (Fig. 3.3) by enabling decentralized model training without the need to share raw data [42]. In FL, local vehicles or traffic sensors train models based on their own data, and only model

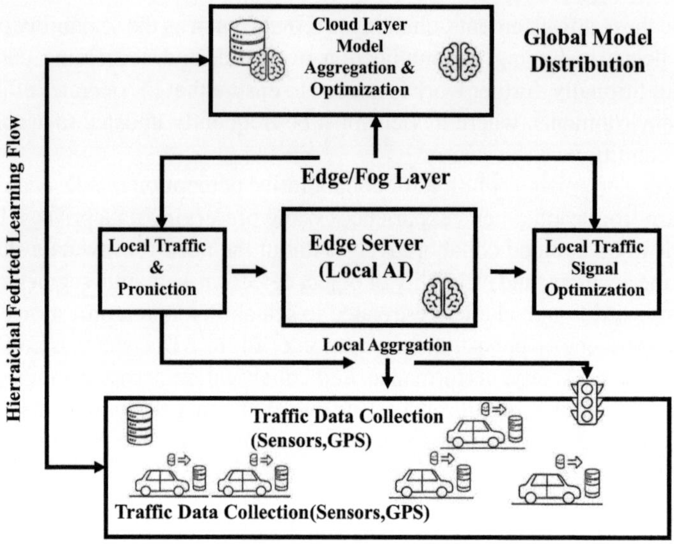

Fig. 3.3 A framework for federated TFP, illustrating local training and global aggregation

updates—such as gradients or weights—are sent to a central server for aggregation. This ensures that sensitive information, like travel routes or driver behavior, remains local, while still enabling collaborative learning across different cities or intersections.

FL facilitates the sharing of predictive models across different locations [25], fostering collaboration between cities, traffic management agencies, or manufacturers. By aggregating local updates from various regions, FL creates a global model that improves prediction accuracy across a broader geographic area. For example, a city with dense traffic data can share insights on congestion patterns, while another city with less data can benefit from the model updates provided by the first city. This approach results in more accurate and generalized predictions, enhancing traffic management at the city or regional level.

Several advanced ML techniques can complement FL-based TFP. One prominent approach is the use of time-series models like Long Short-Term Memory (LSTM) networks [14] and Gated Recurrent Units (GRU) [13]. These models capture temporal dependencies in traffic data, predicting future traffic conditions based on historical patterns. LSTM and GRU networks are particularly well-suited for this task, as they can capture long-term dependencies and mitigate the vanishing gradient problem, a common issue in traditional recurrent neural networks (RNNs).

In addition to time-series models, Graph Neural Networks (GNNs) are increasingly being utilized for traffic prediction tasks involving spatially correlated data, such as road networks. GNNs represent intersections as nodes and roads as edges, effectively capturing the relationships between neighboring intersections. This is particularly useful for modeling traffic conditions in a networked environment, where the traffic at one intersection affects conditions at neighboring intersections. GNN-based FL enables the aggregation of model updates from distributed traffic sensors or vehicles, enhancing collaborative learning while ensuring data privacy.

In intelligent signal control, FL can be combined with reinforcement learning (RL) to create adaptive traffic signal control systems [62]. RL algorithms learn to optimize signal timings based on real-time traffic conditions, while FL enables decentralized training and model updates. By combining FL with RL, adaptive signal control can be implemented across a network of intersections, improving traffic flow and reducing congestion.

Although FL offers significant advantages, it also introduces trade-offs, particularly in terms of accuracy, latency, and communication overhead [28]. FL typically requires transmitting model updates between local clients and a central server, which can lead to communication delays. The size of model updates, especially for complex models like LSTM or GNN, can be large, potentially introducing delays in real-time decision-making. This communication overhead may impact the timeliness of model updates and reduce the effectiveness of real-time traffic control.

Furthermore, the accuracy of FL-based TFPs may fall short compared to traditional centralized methods. Since the model is trained on local data from different locations, it may not always converge to an optimal global model. Non-IID data [63] and heterogeneity across local clients can also influence the performance of federated models. Ensuring efficient convergence and accurate models across diverse environments remains a challenge.

Despite these challenges, FL offers substantial benefits for TFP and intelligent signal control. It allows multiple cities or traffic systems to collaborate without compromising privacy, improving the robustness and generalization of traffic models. By enabling continuous updates to traffic prediction models, FL enhances the responsiveness of intelligent signal control systems, making traffic management more adaptive and efficient. Moreover, the combination of FL with techniques like RL and GNNs [29] holds great promise for enhancing both TFPs and signal control, paving the way for smarter, more sustainable transportation networks.

3.3 Personalized Mobility and Route Recommendation

Personalized mobility, often referred to as Mobility-as-a-Service (MaaS) [21], represents a paradigm shift in how individuals interact with transportation systems. Instead of relying on personal vehicle ownership, MaaS enables users to access a range of transport options—such as buses, taxis, ride-sharing services, bike-sharing, and even electric scooters—through a single platform. The goal is to provide users with a seamless, flexible, and efficient way to plan and execute their journeys based on their specific preferences, needs, and real-time conditions. MaaS aims to enhance the convenience and sustainability of urban mobility while reducing traffic congestion and emissions.

One of the cornerstones of MaaS is the ability to offer personalized services to users [36]. Personalization requires understanding individual preferences and travel patterns, which are inherently tied to sensitive data. A user's travel data contains valuable information, including location history, travel preferences, and trip timings. This data can reveal personal habits, frequent destinations, and preferred modes of transport. For instance, a user may prefer to travel by bike during peak hours but opt for a taxi when the weather is unfavorable. Additionally, data about when and where users travel helps optimize recommendations, such as suggesting faster routes or identifying less crowded transport options. However, this data is also highly sensitive, making privacy protection a key challenge [26] in personalized mobility systems.

In traditional centralized recommendation systems [48], raw user data is often shared with central servers to build comprehensive user profiles. These systems then use algorithms to provide personalized recommendations, such as the best routes or transportation options. However, sharing this data can compromise user privacy, as it can reveal sensitive information about personal travel habits and routines. Moreover, centralized systems are vulnerable to data breaches and can raise concerns about how user data is stored, processed, and shared across different service providers.

FL provides a novel solution [58] to these privacy challenges by allowing users to collaboratively train ML models without sharing their raw data. In the context of personalized mobility, FL enables local user devices (smartphones, apps, or in-car systems) to train models based on individual preferences and travel data, and then send only the model updates—such as gradients or weights—to a central server. This way, the model learns from a diverse set of user data, but without exposing sensitive personal information.

In a typical FL-based architecture for personalized mobility [19] and route recommendation (Fig. 3.4), user devices (such as smartphones or vehicle-mounted apps) act as clients. Each client trains a local model based on the user's individual travel data, which includes location information, preferred routes, and trip durations. For example, a user's local model might learn that they typically prefer avoiding toll roads during their commute or that they tend to use ride-sharing services during weekends.

The server, which aggregates the local model updates from all participating clients, then combines them to improve a global model that can make recommendations for all users. The key advantage of FL is that this global model is informed by a wide variety of user preferences, while still respecting individual privacy. The model is updated incrementally, and sensitive data, such as specific location points or detailed trip histories, are never shared with the server. This decentralized approach allows for a personalized recommendation system while maintaining a high level of privacy.

Through this collaborative training process, FL can generate more accurate recommendations [54]. For example, it can suggest routes that balance user preferences, traffic conditions, and weather data. It can also offer better options for shared mobility services, where users can coordinate their travel with others, reducing both congestion and travel costs. This collaborative learning approach, in which different users contribute to the model without sharing their personal data, not only improves recommendation accuracy but also protects user privacy.

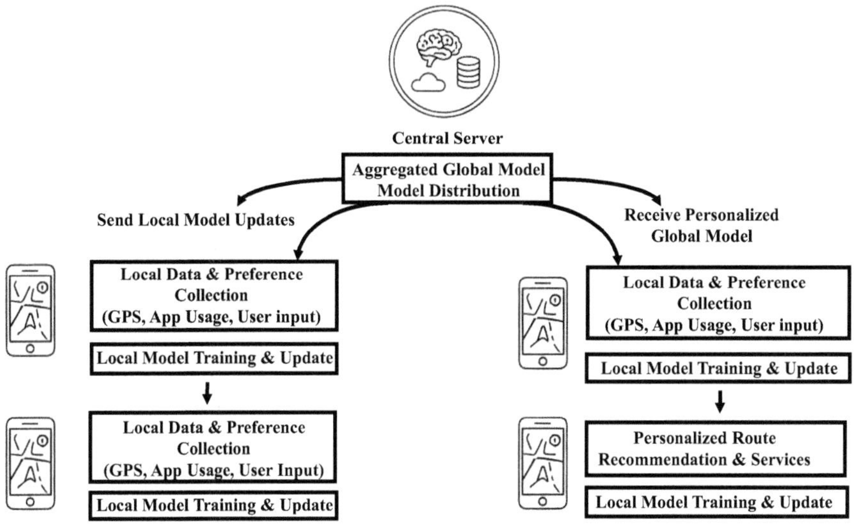

Fig. 3.4 Client-side FL recommendation flowchart, showing the device-server model aggregation loop

FL also addresses the challenges of non-IID data [51], which is common in personalized services like MaaS. In traditional centralized models, training on non-IID data (where users' data may be highly heterogeneous due to differences in travel behavior or preferences) can lead to suboptimal results. FL allows the model to adapt to different data distributions by training locally on each user's data and aggregating the models without requiring the data to be pooled together.

Additionally, FL can be integrated into other mobility services, such as ride-sharing and charging station recommendation systems [33]. In the context of ride-sharing, for example, FL can help improve vehicle dispatch algorithms by learning from the preferences of individual users and providing more efficient ride-matching services. Similarly, for EVs, FL can be used to recommend optimal charging stations [55] based on real-time demand and user location, ensuring that users are always directed to the most convenient and available charging points.

One of the major advantages of FL is its ability to protect user privacy while offering personalized services. By training the model locally, user data remains on the client device, which significantly reduces the risks of data breaches. Moreover, FL supports privacy-enhancing techniques such as DP, which adds noise [57] to the model updates to further obscure individual contributions and prevent inference attacks. This makes FL particularly suitable for sensitive environments like personalized mobility, where data privacy is a key concern.

Despite the numerous advantages, there are also challenges in implementing FL-based systems for personalized mobility. The communication overhead is one such challenge [47]. In a FL setup, each device must periodically send model updates to the central server. This requires significant bandwidth, especially when the models are large, which could lead to delays in updating the global model. Furthermore, devices with limited computational power or network connectivity may not be able to participate in the FL process as efficiently as others.

Another challenge is ensuring model convergence [30] in a FL setting. Because local models are trained on diverse, non-IID data, there may be discrepancies between the local and global models, which could hinder convergence. Techniques such as FedAvg and personalization layers can help mitigate [10] this issue, but they may not fully resolve the challenge in all scenarios.

In terms of performance, FL-based recommendation systems can potentially offer more accurate and timely recommendations than centralized systems. However, these improvements must be carefully balanced with considerations such as model training time, network latency, and the computational power required on user devices. The ultimate success of FL-based systems will depend on optimizing these trade-offs [24] to ensure that users receive the best recommendations in real-time without compromising the user experience.

The application of FL in MaaS and personalized route recommendation holds significant potential for enhancing user satisfaction and privacy protection. As more cities and mobility providers adopt FL models, we can expect increasingly sophisticated and personalized recommendations, which could revolutionize the way we think about urban mobility [64]. The ability to protect user privacy while offering highly personalized and context-aware recommendations will be a key driver of adoption in the MaaS ecosystem.

3.4 Security in V2X and Connected Vehicle Networks

The rise of V2X networks [18] has revolutionized the way vehicles communicate with each other, road infrastructure, and cloud-based services. V2X communication enables real-time data exchange, enhancing safety, traffic management, and overall efficiency. However, this seamless communication also introduces significant security challenges, which must be addressed to ensure the safety and privacy of all parties involved.

One of the key challenges in V2X networks is the highly dynamic topology [46] of the communication environment. Vehicles are in constant motion, and their network connections can change rapidly as they approach or move away from other vehicles, road infrastructure, or cellular towers. This dynamic environment can make it difficult to establish and maintain stable, secure communication channels. In addition, as the number of connected vehicles increases, so does the complexity of the network, leading to potential vulnerabilities in communication protocols.

Another critical challenge is the authentication of the entities [45] involved in communication. In a V2X network, it is crucial to verify the identity of vehicles, infrastructure, and other devices to prevent unauthorized access or communication. Without robust authentication mechanisms, attackers could impersonate legitimate vehicles or infrastructure components, leading to malicious activities such as spoofing, data breaches, and DoS attacks. The risk of such attacks is heightened by the absence of a centralized control point, which makes it harder to manage trust and enforce security policies across a decentralized network.

Data tampering is also a significant concern [40] in V2X networks. Vehicles and infrastructure components rely on data exchanges for a variety of tasks, including navigation, traffic management, and safety features. If this data is intercepted or altered during transmission, it can lead to catastrophic consequences. For instance, if an attacker modifies the traffic signal data or sends false vehicle position information, it could cause accidents or traffic congestion. Ensuring the integrity and authenticity of the data exchanged within the network is essential to prevent such attacks.

FL offers a promising solution to address these security challenges in V2X networks. FL allows the decentralized training of ML models on the devices of individual vehicles, while only sharing model updates with a central server rather than raw data. This approach ensures that sensitive vehicle data, such as location and behavior patterns, remains private. In the context of V2X security, FL can be applied to enhance IDS [53] by enabling vehicles to detect malicious activities without exposing their private data.

A federated IDS based on FL (Fig. 3.5) works by training local models on the devices of individual vehicles or RSUs. These models can identify abnormal behavior or unauthorized activities, such as an attacker attempting to spoof vehicle identities or inject false data into the network. Once local models are trained, they can share their insights with the central server, which aggregates the information to refine a global model. This global model can then be used to detect and prevent new, previously unseen attacks.

Additionally, FL can be used to detect abnormal behavior [3] and identify malicious nodes within the V2X network. By analyzing the behavior of connected vehicles and infrastructure components, FL-based models can identify patterns of communication that deviate from normal operation, indicating the presence of a malicious

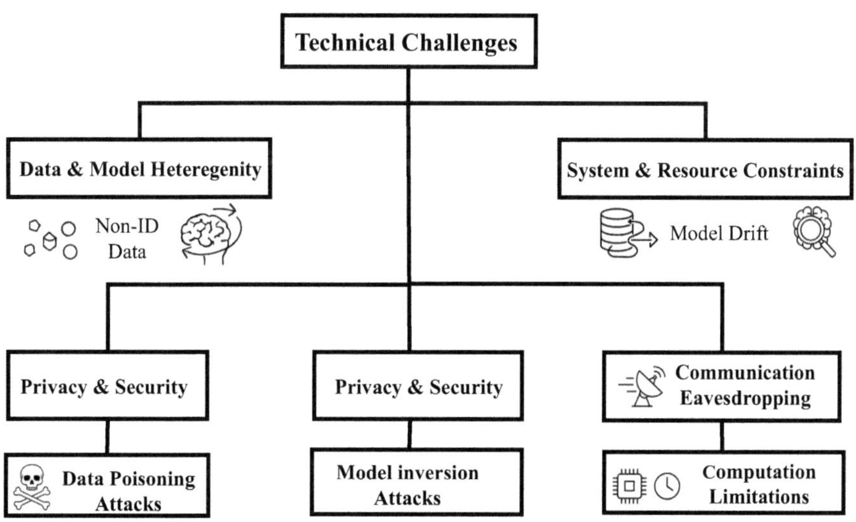

Fig. 3.5 Architecture of a FL-based IDS for V2X networks

actor. This capability is particularly important in dynamic V2X networks, where attackers may attempt to exploit vulnerabilities in real-time communication to launch attacks, such as jamming or flooding the network with fake messages.

Another important application of FL in V2X security is in the area of SecAgg and model protection mechanisms. In FL, multiple devices collaborate to train a shared model without sharing raw data. However, this also introduces the risk of model poisoning [12], where an attacker could inject malicious updates into the model during the aggregation process. To mitigate this risk, SecAgg protocols can be employed, ensuring that model updates are encrypted and only accessible to the central server in an aggregated form, thus preventing attackers from manipulating the model. Additionally, privacy-preserving techniques, such as DP, can be incorporated into the FL framework to further protect the model from malicious influence.

To enhance trust and security in V2X networks, FL can be combined with blockchain [16] or encryption mechanisms. Blockchain, with its inherent properties of immutability and decentralization, can provide a secure and transparent way to log communication events and model updates. In a V2X network, blockchain can be used to record vehicle transactions, such as data exchanges and authentication events, ensuring that all actions are verifiable and tamper-proof. This can significantly enhance trust between different entities in the network, as well as provide an auditable trail of actions that can be reviewed in case of security incidents.

Encryption mechanisms, such as HE [9] or secure multi-party computation [38], can also be integrated into FL models to further protect the privacy of vehicle data. These encryption techniques allow data to be processed in its encrypted form, ensuring that sensitive information, such as vehicle locations or driver behavior, is never exposed during the learning process. By combining FL with encryption, V2X networks can benefit from both improved security and enhanced privacy, ensuring that data is protected from unauthorized access and tampering.

While FL offers many advantages in terms of enhancing security in V2X networks, there are also challenges related to system complexity and real-time constraints. The decentralized nature of FL means that model updates must be transmitted between a large number of vehicles and infrastructure components, which can introduce significant communication overhead. As the number of connected vehicles grows, the volume of data exchanged for model updates can become overwhelming, potentially leading to delays in model aggregation and updates. Additionally, the training of complex ML models on resource-constrained devices, such as in-vehicle systems, can increase computational requirements and impact the real-time performance [31] of the network.

To address these challenges, lightweight ML algorithms [15] and communication-efficient FL protocols can be employed to reduce the communication overhead [47] and computational load. Techniques such as model pruning [34], quantization, and edge aggregation [56] can help improve the efficiency of FL in V2X networks, making it more suitable for real-time applications.

In conclusion, V2X networks face significant security challenges, including high dynamic topologies, identity authentication issues, and the risk of data tampering. FL offers a promising solution by enabling decentralized training of security models while preserving data privacy. FL can be used to enhance intrusion detection, detect malicious nodes, and secure model aggregation in V2X networks. Additionally, combining FL with blockchain and encryption mechanisms can further enhance trust and security in these networks. However, the complexity of the system and the need for real-time performance pose significant challenges that need to be addressed through efficient protocols and lightweight models. The future of V2X security will depend on the continued integration of FL, encryption, and blockchain to create secure, scalable, and privacy-preserving communication systems for connected vehicles.

3.5 Energy-Efficient and Sustainable Mobility

As ITS evolve globally, the growing energy consumption and carbon emissions [22] associated with these systems have become pressing issues. Vehicles, infrastructure, communication networks, and data centers all contribute significantly to the overall energy usage. Addressing these challenges is essential for achieving a more sustainable and efficient transportation ecosystem. FL, as an innovative distributed ML technique, holds great potential in optimizing energy efficiency [28] and promoting sustainable mobility. This section explores the energy consumption challenges in ITS, the role of FL in energy optimization, and its contribution to sustainable development goals (SDGs) [4].

Energy consumption in ITS arises from multiple sources, including vehicles, communication infrastructure, and computational resources. To provide a unified view, the total energy consumption $\mathcal{E}_{\text{total}}$ of an ITS-assisted FL system can be expressed as:

$$\mathcal{E}_{\text{total}} = \sum_{i=1}^{N} \left(\mathcal{E}_i^{\text{comp}} + \mathcal{E}_i^{\text{comm}} + \mathcal{E}_i^{\text{infra}}\right), \tag{3.1}$$

where $\mathcal{E}_i^{\text{comp}}$ represents the computational energy consumed [2] by the ith device during local training, $\mathcal{E}_i^{\text{comm}}$ denotes the communication energy required for transmitting model updates, and $\mathcal{E}_i^{\text{infra}}$ captures the static energy consumed by supporting infrastructure such as RSUs and gateways. This expression highlights that energy efficiency in ITS requires joint optimization across computation, communication, and infrastructure layers.

A major portion of total energy expenditure comes from vehicular and edge computation. The energy consumed by a single device during one local update round can be formulated as:

$$\mathcal{E}_i^{\text{comp}} = \kappa_i C_i D_i f_i^2, \tag{3.2}$$

where κ_i is the effective capacitance coefficient of the device's processor, C_i is the number of CPU cycles required per sample, D_i is the number of local data samples, and f_i denotes the CPU frequency. This quadratic relationship with f_i shows that computational energy increases rapidly with processing speed, implying the need for adaptive frequency scaling to balance energy and latency.

In addition to computation, communication also constitutes a major portion of total power consumption, especially in large-scale vehicular networks. The communication energy per transmission can be expressed as:

$$\mathcal{E}_i^{\text{comm}} = P_i^{\text{tx}} \cdot \frac{S_i}{R_i}, \tag{3.3}$$

where P_i^{tx} is the transmit power, S_i is the size of the transmitted model update (in bits), and R_i represents the achievable data rate determined by channel bandwidth and signal-to-noise ratio (SNR). This equation indicates that reducing model size or improving transmission rate can effectively lower communication energy consumption.

To achieve sustainability, the optimization objective in FL-based ITS can be formulated as a multi-objective problem [61] that jointly minimizes energy consumption and learning loss:

$$\min_{\{w_i\}} \alpha \sum_{i=1}^{N} \left(\mathcal{E}_i^{\text{comp}} + \mathcal{E}_i^{\text{comm}}\right) + (1-\alpha)\mathcal{L}_{\text{global}}, \tag{3.4}$$

where $\mathcal{L}_{\text{global}}$ is the global model loss aggregated from all devices, and $\alpha \in [0, 1]$ is a weighting factor balancing energy efficiency and model performance. When α is high, the optimization favors energy saving, while smaller α emphasizes accuracy.

To further promote sustainability, FL can be extended to support dynamic task scheduling and energy-aware aggregation. In such cases, the system dynamically adjusts resource allocation across devices and communication links to minimize total system energy. The energy efficiency ratio η_{eff} can be defined as:

$$\eta_{\text{eff}} = \frac{\Delta\mathcal{L}_{\text{global}}}{\mathcal{E}_{\text{total}}}, \tag{3.5}$$

where $\Delta\mathcal{L}_{\text{global}}$ represents the improvement in model performance (e.g., accuracy gain) per unit of energy consumed. A higher η_{eff} indicates more energy-efficient learning [5], serving as a critical performance metric for energy-aware FL.

In practical implementations, FL supports several sustainability-oriented applications in ITS:

- **Electric Vehicle Energy Management** [49]: Vehicles collaboratively train models to optimize charging schedules and energy distribution without revealing private data. Each vehicle i minimizes its local energy loss $\mathcal{L}_i^{\text{EV}}$ subject to battery and charging constraints:

$$\min_{\theta_i} \mathcal{L}_i^{\text{EV}} = \|E_i^{\text{pred}}(\theta_i) - E_i^{\text{real}}\|^2, \tag{3.6}$$

where E_i^{pred} and E_i^{real} denote the predicted and actual energy usage respectively, and θ_i represents model parameters for vehicle i.

- **Traffic Flow Optimization**: FL can be used to collaboratively minimize total congestion delay while reducing carbon emissions:

$$\min_{\Theta} \sum_{r \in \mathcal{R}} (\lambda_1 T_r + \lambda_2 C_r), \tag{3.7}$$

where T_r is the average delay on route r, C_r is the estimated carbon emission, and λ_1, λ_2 are trade-off coefficients controlling delay and emission priorities.

- **Green FL**: Energy-awareness is introduced directly into the learning process by adjusting the aggregation frequency τ_e to balance energy and accuracy:

$$\tau_e^* = \arg\min_{\tau_e} \left(\mathcal{E}_{\text{total}}(\tau_e) + \lambda_f \mathcal{L}_{\text{global}}(\tau_e) \right), \tag{3.8}$$

where λ_f is a penalty coefficient reflecting the trade-off between energy cost and model convergence speed.

These formulations illustrate how FL can not only enhance learning efficiency but also act as an enabler for sustainable and energy-aware mobility. In particular, Green FL emphasizes minimizing the environmental footprint by leveraging renewable-powered edge nodes, adaptive communication, and resource-efficient model updates.

In conclusion, FL provides a viable path toward energy-efficient and sustainable mobility in ITS. By decentralizing computation and intelligently scheduling communication, FL minimizes overall energy consumption while maintaining system performance. The integration of energy-awareness into FL—particularly in the form of Green FL—supports both technological advancement and global sustainability objectives, enabling ITS to achieve lower carbon emissions, higher efficiency, and longer operational lifetimes.

Summary

This chapter explored five key application areas in ITS: **AD and Cooperative Perception**, **TFP and Intelligent Signal Control**, **Personalized Mobility and Route Recommendation**, **Security in V2X and Connected Vehicle Networks**, and **Energy-Efficient and Sustainable Mobility**. These areas, while distinct in their focus, share several common themes that drive the advancement of smart mobility solutions.

First, **multi-source data collaboration** emerged as a critical element across all applications. Whether in AD, TFP, or energy management, leveraging diverse data sources—such as vehicle sensors, traffic infrastructure, and environmental data—enables more robust and accurate decision-making. Effective data fusion enhances system intelligence, leading to optimized performance and more reliable predictions.

Second, the **balance between privacy protection and system performance** is a recurring challenge. In applications such as cooperative perception and V2X communications, the need to protect sensitive information while maintaining high performance is paramount. FL plays a significant role in addressing this challenge by enabling decentralized learning and model training, which preserves privacy while still optimizing system capabilities. Each application highlighted the importance of adopting privacy-preserving techniques to ensure user trust and regulatory compliance.

Lastly, the chapter emphasized the growing trend of **intelligent and sustainable systems** in ITS. From energy-efficient mobility solutions to personalized route recommendations, the integration of AI and ML technologies is transforming transportation systems into more adaptive and sustainable environments. The exploration of energy-efficient and sustainable mobility particularly underscored the role of FL in reducing energy consumption while promoting environmental sustainability.

These applications discussed in this chapter illustrate the potential of ITS to address modern mobility challenges. Through the collaborative use of data, privacy-aware techniques, and sustainable design principles, ITS can continue to evolve into more efficient, secure, and environmentally-friendly systems.

References

1. Aoki, S., Higuchi, T., Altintas, O.: Cooperative perception with deep reinforcement learning for connected vehicles. In: 2020 IEEE Intelligent Vehicles Symposium (IV), pp. 328–334. IEEE (2020)
2. Asim, M., Wang, Y., Wang, K., Huang, P.Q.: A review on computational intelligence techniques in cloud and edge computing. IEEE Trans. Emerg. Top. Comput. Intell. **4**(6), 742–763 (2020)
3. Baccari, S., Hadded, M., Ghazzai, H., Touati, H., Elhadef, M.: Anomaly detection in connected and autonomous vehicles: a survey, analysis, and research challenges. IEEE Access **12**, 19250–19276 (2024)
4. Banister, D.: The sustainable mobility paradigm. Transp. Policy **15**(2), 73–80 (2008)
5. Bergstra, J., Bardenet, R., Bengio, Y., Kégl, B.: Algorithms for hyper-parameter optimization. Adv. Neural Inf. Proces. Syst. **24** (2011)
6. Bojarski, M., Del Testa, D., Dworakowski, D., Firner, B., Flepp, B., Goyal, P., Jackel, L.D., Monfort, M., Muller, U., Zhang, J., et al.: End to End Learning for Self-driving Cars (2016). arXiv:1604.07316
7. Chen, C., Seff, A., Kornhauser, A., Xiao, J.: Deepdriving: learning affordance for direct perception in autonomous driving. In: Proceedings of the IEEE International Conference on Computer Vision, pp. 2722–2730 (2015)
8. Chen, L.C., Papandreou, G., Kokkinos, I., Murphy, K., Yuille, A.L.: Deeplab: Semantic image segmentation with deep convolutional nets, atrous convolution, and fully connected crfs. IEEE Trans. Pattern Anal. Mach. Intell. **40**(4), 834–848 (2017)
9. Cheon, J.H., Kim, A., Kim, M., Song, Y.: Homomorphic encryption for arithmetic of approximate numbers. In: International Conference on the Theory and Application of Cryptology and Information Security, pp. 409–437. Springer, Berlin (2017)
10. Fallah, A., Mokhtari, A., Ozdaglar, A.: Personalized federated learning with theoretical guarantees: a model-agnostic meta-learning approach. Adv. Neural. Inf. Process. Syst. **33**, 3557–3568 (2020)

11. Fan, R., Guo, S., Bocus, M.J.: Autonomous Driving Perception. Springer, Cham, Switzerland (2023)
12. Fung, C., Yoon, C.J., Beschastnikh, I.: The limitations of federated learning in sybil settings. In: 23rd International Symposium on Research in Attacks, Intrusions and Defenses (RAID 2020), pp. 301–316 (2020)
13. Gao, Y., Glowacka, D.: Deep gate recurrent neural network. In: Asian Conference on Machine Learning, pp. 350–365. PMLR (2016)
14. Hochreiter, S., Schmidhuber, J.: Long short-term memory. Neural Comput. **9**(8), 1735–1780 (1997)
15. Howard, A.G., Zhu, M., Chen, B., Kalenichenko, D., Wang, W., Weyand, T., Andreetto, M., Adam, H.: Mobilenets: efficient convolutional neural networks for mobile vision applications (2017). arXiv:1704.04861
16. Hua, G., Zhu, L., Wu, J., Shen, C., Zhou, L., Lin, Q.: Blockchain-based federated learning for intelligent control in heavy haul railway. IEEE Access **8**, 176830–176839 (2020)
17. Huang, K., Shi, B., Li, X., Li, X., Huang, S., Li, Y.: Multi-modal sensor fusion for auto driving perception: a survey (2022). arXiv:2202.02703
18. Hussein, N.H., Yaw, C.T., Koh, S.P., Tiong, S.K., Chong, K.H.: A comprehensive survey on vehicular networking: communications, applications, challenges, and upcoming research directions. IEEE Access **10**, 86127–86180 (2022)
19. Javeed, D., Saeed, M.S., Kumar, P., Jolfaei, A., Islam, S., Islam, A.N.: Federated learning-based personalized recommendation systems: an overview on security and privacy challenges. IEEE Trans. Consum. Electron. **70**(1), 2618–2627 (2023)
20. Jiang, W., Luo, J.: Graph neural network for traffic forecasting: a survey. Expert Syst. Appl. **207**, 117921 (2022)
21. Jittrapirom, P., Caiati, V., Feneri, A.M., Ebrahimigharehbaghi, S., Alonso-González, M.J., Narayan, J.: Mobility as a service: a critical review of definitions, assessments of schemes, and key challenges. Urban Plann. **2**(2), 13–25 (2017)
22. Juang, P., Oki, H., Wang, Y., Martonosi, M., Peh, L.S., Rubenstein, D.: Energy-efficient computing for wildlife tracking: Design tradeoffs and early experiences with zebranet. In: Proceedings of the 10th International Conference on Architectural Support for Programming Languages and Operating Systems, pp. 96–107 (2002)
23. Jung, H.Y., Paek, D.H., Kong, S.H.: Open-source autonomous driving software platforms: comparison of autoware and apollo (2025). arXiv:2501.18942
24. Kairouz, P., McMahan, H.B., Avent, B., Bellet, A., Bennis, M., Bhagoji, A.N., Bonawitz, K., Charles, Z., Cormode, G., Cummings, R., et al.: Advances and open problems in federated learning. Found. Trends® Mach. Learn. **14**(1–2), 1–210 (2021)
25. Kaur, G., Grewal, S.K., Jain, A.: Federated learning based spatio-temporal framework for real-time traffic prediction. Wirel. Pers. Commun. **136**(2), 849–865 (2024)
26. Keerthana, P., Kavitha, M., Subburaj, J.: Privacy preservation in federated learning. In: Federated Learning, pp. 127–144. CRC Press (2024)
27. Kendall, A., Hawke, J., Janz, D., Mazur, P., Reda, D., Allen, J.M., Lam, V.D., Bewley, A., Shah, A.: Learning to drive in a day. In: 2019 International Conference on Robotics and Automation (ICRA), pp. 8248–8254. IEEE (2019)
28. Konečný, J., McMahan, H.B., Yu, F.X., Richtárik, P., Suresh, A.T., Bacon, D.: Federated learning: strategies for improving communication efficiency (2016). arXiv:1610.05492
29. Li, M., Pan, X., Liu, C., Li, Z.: Federated deep reinforcement learning-based urban traffic signal optimal control. Sci. Rep. **15**(1), 11724 (2025)
30. Li, X., Jiang, M., Zhang, X., Kamp, M., Dou, Q.: Fedbn: federated learning on non-iid features via local batch normalization (2021). arXiv:2102.07623
31. Liu, G.: Real-Time Object Detection for Autonomous Driving Based on Deep Learning. Texas A&M University-Corpus Christi (2017). Master's thesis
32. Liu, W., Anguelov, D., Erhan, D., Szegedy, C., Reed, S., Fu, C.Y., Berg, A.C.: Ssd: Single shot multibox detector. In: European Conference on Computer Vision, pp. 21–37. Springer, Berlin (2016)

33. Liu, Y., James, J., Kang, J., Niyato, D., Zhang, S.: Privacy-preserving traffic flow prediction: a federated learning approach. IEEE Internet Things J. **7**(8), 7751–7763 (2020)
34. Liu, Z., Sun, M., Zhou, T., Huang, G., Darrell, T.: Rethinking the value of network pruning (2018). arXiv:1810.05270
35. Lv, Y., Duan, Y., Kang, W., Li, Z., Wang, F.Y.: Traffic flow prediction with big data: a deep learning approach. IEEE Trans. Intell. Transp. Syst. **16**(2), 865–873 (2014)
36. Lyons, G.: Getting smart about urban mobility-aligning the paradigms of smart and sustainable. Transp. Res. Part A: Policy Practice **115**, 4–14 (2018)
37. McMahan, B., Moore, E., Ramage, D., Hampson, S., y Arcas, B.A.: Communication-efficient learning of deep networks from decentralized data. In: Artificial Intelligence and Statistics, pp. 1273–1282. PMLR (2017)
38. Mugunthan, V., Polychroniadou, A., Byrd, D., Balch, T.H.: Smpai: secure multi-party computation for federated learning. In: Proceedings of the NeurIPS 2019 Workshop on Robust AI in Financial Services, vol. 21. MIT Press Cambridge, MA, USA (2019)
39. Nguyen, A., Do, T., Tran, M., Nguyen, B.X., Duong, C., Phan, T., Tjiputra, E., Tran, Q.D.: Deep federated learning for autonomous driving. In: 2022 IEEE Intelligent Vehicles Symposium (IV), pp. 1824–1830. IEEE (2022)
40. Obaidat, M., Khodjaeva, M., Holst, J., Ben Zid, M.: Security and privacy challenges in vehicular ad hoc networks. In: Connected Vehicles in the Internet of Things: Concepts, Technologies and Frameworks for the IoV, pp. 223–251. Springer, Berlin (2020)
41. Pandya, S., Srivastava, G., Jhaveri, R., Babu, M.R., Bhattacharya, S., Maddikunta, P.K.R., Mastorakis, S., Piran, M.J., Gadekallu, T.R.: Federated learning for smart cities: a comprehensive survey. Sustain. Energy Technol. Assess. **55**, 102987 (2023)
42. Pei, J., Feng, J.: Federated cognitive learning for next generation recommendation system. IEEE Consum. Electron. Mag. (2024)
43. Pei, J., Li, W.: Dual model pruning enables efficient federated learning in intelligent transportation systems. IEEE Trans. Intell. Transp. Syst. (2024a)
44. Pei, J., Li, W.: Unveiling the effects of slightly skewed labels on traffic data analysis. IEEE Trans. Intell. Transp. Syst. (2024b)
45. Qu, F., Wu, Z., Wang, F.Y., Cho, W.: A security and privacy review of vanets. IEEE Trans. Intell. Transp. Syst. **16**(6), 2985–2996 (2015)
46. Rajaraman, R.: Topology control and routing in ad hoc networks: a survey. ACM SIGACT News **33**(2), 60–73 (2002)
47. Reisizadeh, A., Mokhtari, A., Hassani, H., Jadbabaie, A., Pedarsani, R.: Fedpaq: a communication-efficient federated learning method with periodic averaging and quantization. In: International Conference on Artificial Intelligence and Statistics, pp. 2021–2031. PMLR (2020)
48. Ricci, F., Rokach, L., Shapira, B.: Introduction to recommender systems handbook. In: Recommender Systems Handbook, pp. 1–35. Springer, Berlin (2010)
49. Shin, M., Choi, D.H., Kim, J.: Cooperative management for pv/ess-enabled electric vehicle charging stations: a multiagent deep reinforcement learning approach. IEEE Trans. Industr. Inf. **16**(5), 3493–3503 (2019)
50. Shokri, R., Stronati, M., Song, C., Shmatikov, V.: Membership inference attacks against machine learning models. In: 2017 IEEE Symposium on Security and Privacy (SP), pp. 3–18. IEEE (2017)
51. Tan, Y., Long, G., Liu, L., Zhou, T., Lu, Q., Jiang, J., Zhang, C.: Fedproto: federated prototype learning across heterogeneous clients. Proc. AAAI Conf. Artif. Intell. **36**, 8432–8440 (2022)
52. Teichmann, M., Weber, M., Zoellner, M., Cipolla, R., Urtasun, R.: Multinet: Real-time joint semantic reasoning for autonomous driving. In: 2018 IEEE Intelligent Vehicles Symposium (IV), pp. 1013–1020. IEEE (2018)
53. Tham, C.K., Yang, L., Khanna, A., Gera, B.: Federated learning for anomaly detection in vehicular networks. In: 2023 IEEE 97th Vehicular Technology Conference (VTC2023-Spring), pp. 1–6. IEEE (2023)

54. Vyas, J., Das, D., Chaudhury, S., et al.: Federated learning based driver recommendation for next generation transportation system. Expert Syst. Appl. **225**, 119951 (2023)
55. Wang, X., Zheng, X., Liang, X.: Charging station recommendation for electric vehicle based on federated learning. J. Phys. Conf. Ser. **1792**, 012055 (2021) (IOP Publishing)
56. Wang, Y., Zeng, Z.: Data-Driven Solutions to Transportation Problems. Elsevier (2018)
57. Wei, K., Li, J., Ding, M., Ma, C., Yang, H.H., Farokhi, F., Jin, S., Quek, T.Q., Poor, H.V.: Federated learning with differential privacy: algorithms and performance analysis. IEEE Trans. Inf. Forensics Secur. **15**, 3454–3469 (2020)
58. Yang, Q., Liu, Y., Chen, T., Tong, Y.: Federated machine learning: concept and applications. ACM Trans. Intell. Syst. Technol. (TIST) **10**(2), 1–19 (2019)
59. Yu, Z., Pei, J., Zhu, M., Zhang, J., Li, J.: Multi-attribute adaptive aggregation transformer for vehicle re-identification. Inf. Process. Manag. **59**(2), 102868 (2022)
60. Zhang, R., Mao, J., Wang, H., Li, B., Cheng, X., Yang, L.: A survey on federated learning in intelligent transportation systems. IEEE Trans. Intell. Veh. (2024)
61. Zhang, Y., Yang, Q.: An overview of multi-task learning. Natl. Sci. Rev. **5**(1), 30–43 (2018)
62. Zhao, H., Dong, C., Cao, J., Chen, Q.: A survey on deep reinforcement learning approaches for traffic signal control. Eng. Appl. Artif. Intell. **133**, 108100 (2024)
63. Zhu, H., Xu, J., Liu, S., Jin, Y.: Federated learning on non-iid data: a survey. Neurocomputing **465**, 371–390 (2021)
64. Zmud, J., Ecola, L., Phleps, P., Feige, I.: The future of mobility: scenarios for the United States in 2030. RR-246-ifmo (2013)

Chapter 4
Case Studies and Research Insights

Abstract This chapter provided a comparative analysis of academic breakthroughs and industrial practices in Federated Learning (FL) for smart mobility via key case studies. Academic research (Sect. 4.1) has focused on solving specific hard problems: FADNet was designed to overcome Non-IID data challenges in vehicular perception; the FedGRU scheme was proposed to handle spatio-temporal heterogeneity in traffic flow prediction (TFP); and Byzantine-robust aggregators were developed to secure open V2X networks. In contrast, industrial practice (Sect. 4.2) is driven by real-world "pain points": Tesla's "Shadow Mode" represents a pragmatic data loop balancing cost and efficiency; Baidu's Apollo platform employs FL as a governance tool to break "data silos" between competing OEMs and government; and Huawei's V2X solution highlights robustness as a fundamental prerequisite for deploying distributed security (IDS). The comparative analysis (Sect. 4.3) revealed a key gap between academia (pursuing "model optimality") and industry (pursuing "system viability") in performance, privacy, and deployment strategies. A core trend emerged: FL is currently used primarily as an "offline optimization" tool rather than for "real-time online learning," and it relies heavily on complex hybrid architectures like Vehicle-Edge-Cloud (V-E-C). The real-world bottlenecks in heterogeneity, scalability, and governance revealed in this chapter establish the foundation for the discussion of future challenges in Chap. 5.

Keywords FL · Case studies · Industrial practices · Autonomous driving · Traffic flow prediction · V2X security · Byzantine-robust · Data silos · Shadow mode · Vehicle-edge-cloud

4.1 Academic Research Review

The academic landscape for FL in smart mobility has evolved from theoretical exploration to deep, vertical-specific practice. FL is no longer just a general-purpose privacy tool; it has given rise to targeted solutions for the specific challenges inherent in ITS.

© The Author(s), under exclusive license to Springer Nature Singapore Pte Ltd. 2026
J. Pei et al., *Federated Learning for Smart Mobility*, SpringerBriefs in Computer Science,
https://doi.org/10.1007/978-981-95-6160-5_4

This section refrains from a broad literature survey. Instead, it offers a deep analysis of three representative and high-impact research directions that correspond to the three most critical challenges in smart mobility: **perception**, **prediction**, and **security**. We analyze these studies as distinct cases, detailing their methodologies and contributions. These academic breakthroughs provide the necessary "toolbox" for solving the real-world industrial bottlenecks that will be discussed in Sect. 4.2.

4.1.1 Case 1: Vehicular Federated Learning (VFL) for Perception and Privacy

As AD emerges as one of the most transformative goals within ITS, "end-to-end" deep learning has become a primary technological path explored by the industry. This approach, as demonstrated in many cutting-edge systems, involves training a single deep neural network to directly map raw sensor inputs (like camera images) to driving control commands (such as steering angles). This method discards traditional, complex, rules-based modular systems, instead entrusting the driving decisions entirely to a data-driven AI model.

The implementation of this method is critically dependent on massive and diverse real-world training data. To acquire this data, the industry-standard "Centralized Local Learning" (CLL) paradigm requires uploading all raw data collected by the fleet—including video streams, radar readings, and GPS trajectories—to a central cloud server for centralized processing and training.

This centralized data strategy faces two fundamental and nearly insurmountable obstacles in practice. First, it introduces **severe data privacy and security risks**. A vehicle's driving trajectories and captured raw camera footage are highly sensitive personal data; centrally sharing this data with third parties (like car manufacturers or service providers) constitutes a "serious violation of user privacy." Second, this strategy faces **increasingly stringent regulatory hurdles**. Under strict global data sovereignty regulations like the EU's GDPR or China's Data Security Law, the large-scale, cross-border transfer of raw vehicle data has become extremely difficult and fraught with risk.

This has directly spurred the rise of the specialized field of **VFL**. The core philosophy of VFL is "moving the model, not the data." The model is sent down to each device (vehicle) to be trained on local data, while the raw data itself remains localized and never leaves the vehicle. This paradigm, in theory, perfectly resolves the privacy and compliance challenges of AD training.

The application of VFL to the complex, real-world scenario of AD, however, immediately introduces two new, equally difficult technical challenges. The first challenge stems from the **central server bottleneck**. Standard "Server-based Federated Learning" (SFL) relies on a central server to coordinate all vehicles, distribute models, and aggregate updates. In an AD context, when the network needs to scale to millions of vehicles, this central server instantly becomes a massive "communication bottleneck" and a "single point of failure," which is unacceptable for a safety-critical transportation system.

The second challenge is more fundamental: **Non-IID data**. This is one of the most central problems in FL. In AD, the Non-IID problem is particularly extreme: each vehicle's data distribution is unique and severely imbalanced. Data collected by a vehicle in urban traffic congestion is entirely different from data gathered on a dimly lit rural road. Forcibly averaging the local models trained on such heterogeneous data leads to a global model with massive variance, severely degraded performance, and potential failure to converge. Therefore, the true challenge facing the AD industry is: Is it possible to achieve a high-performance, scalable, and privacy-preserving VFL training framework by completely discarding the central server for a fully decentralized (P2P) architecture, while simultaneously designing a specialized neural network capable of efficiently handling extreme Non-IID data?

It was this urgent need that led to a complete solution proposed by academic research, designed specifically to address all the aforementioned challenges. This solution is a synergistic innovation at both the "framework" and "network" levels. First, to solve the "central server bottleneck," the research introduced a **"peer-to-peer Deep Federated Learning (DFL)"** framework [5]. This is a "fully decentralized" topology where vehicles (referred to as "silos") communicate and aggregate models directly with each other via a pre-computed "Overlay Graph," completely eliminating the central server and thus circumventing the "single point of failure" and communication bottleneck risks. More critically, to overcome the "Non-IID data" hurdle, the researchers recognized that traditional network architectures perform poorly in FL training. They therefore designed a novel neural network architecture specifically for this task: the **"Federated AD Network" (FADNet)**. The core design of FADNet is a **"dual-path feature extraction"** system, purpose-built to handle the "high variance" problem caused by heterogeneous data. The network first uses an **Input Layer Normalization** to "iron out" the disparate input images from different vehicles. Subsequently, feature extraction is split into two paths: a "**main path**" using standard residual blocks (ResBlock) to extract detailed features for steering prediction—the primary source of model performance but sensitive to Non-IID data; and a "**stable support path**" that runs a "Global Average Pooling" (GAP) layer in parallel with each ResBlock. GAP layers are "non-weighted" layers, meaning they are *not* affected by the weight variance problem during aggregation. The stable features from this "support path" are fed into a specialized "**Accumulation Layer**" and finally combined with the "main path's" detailed features in an "**Aggregation Layer**." In short, FADNet uses a parallel, variance-resistant "support stream" to stabilize and calibrate the "main stream," making its architecture inherently resilient to the shock of Non-IID data.

The study validated its method on three highly challenging datasets: the real-world Udacity dataset, the simulated Carla dataset with diverse weather and lighting, and the indoor Gazebo dataset. The experimental results (measured by RMSE, lower is better) were highly persuasive: the performance of FADNet + DFL was not only superior to other baselines but also **significantly outperformed (outperforms) the**

privacy-violating "CLL" DroNet model. For example, on the most complex Carla dataset, the centralized DroNet achieved an RMSE of 0.333, while FADNet+DFL achieved only 0.203. Ablation studies further confirmed that the P2P DFL framework was superior to the SFL framework, and that the FADNet architecture vastly outperformed DroNet in FL training, proving its specialized design was necessary. Furthermore, the system demonstrated excellent **scalability**: in tests, even when the number of vehicles (silos) was doubled from 11 (Gaia topology) to 22 (NWS topology), the performance of FADNet+DFL remained "highly stable" with almost no degradation.

This research provides an essential practical blueprint for the application of VFL in AD perception. It not only fundamentally solves the **privacy and data compliance issues** of end-to-end AD learning via a fully decentralized DFL framework but also circumvents the **bottleneck risks** of a central server through its P2P topology. Most critically, it successfully tackles the most difficult challenge in FL—**Non-IID data heterogeneity** and model convergence—through the specialized FADNet architecture. This work powerfully demonstrates that **FL is not merely a "performance compromise" made for the sake of privacy**. With careful co-design, the performance of FADNet + DFL ultimately "surpassed" that of traditional, non-private centralized training methods, proving that VFL is not just a privacy tool, but a viable, secure, and high-performance paradigm for AD perception.

4.1.2 Case 2: TFP with Heterogeneous Data

As ITS mature and urbanization accelerates, accurate **TFP** has become a core requirement for modern urban management. It provides the foundational support for alleviating traffic congestion, optimizing traffic signal timing, and enhancing the efficiency of navigation systems. Achieving high-precision predictions requires AI models to rely on massive, multi-source traffic data. In reality, this data is extremely fragmented, dispersed across different **"data silos."** For example, government transportation departments possess data from road sensors and surveillance cameras, while private companies (like DiDi, Uber, or logistics fleets) hold massive, highly valuable proprietary GPS trajectory data.

This "data silo" dilemma, rooted in fierce **commercial competition**, **severe privacy leakage risks**, and increasingly stringent legal compliance (like GDPR), makes traditional centralized data aggregation methods impractical. The application of FL to the specific domain of TFP, however, immediately introduces two unique and significant challenges. First, the TFP task relies heavily on complex temporal models (like GRU or LSTM) to capture traffic dynamics, and these models are typically parameter-heavy. In a federated framework, this translates to **"expensive communication overhead,"** as bulky model updates must be frequently transmitted between clients, easily creating system bottlenecks. Second, the pervasive problem of **statistical heterogeneity (non-IID) data** manifests in TFP as a unique "spatio-temporal" heterogeneity. Data patterns collected by organizations in different geographical locations (e.g., downtown vs. suburban traffic) are vastly different. This discrepancy "violates the i.i.d. assumption commonly used in distributed optimization" and can severely degrade the aggregated global model's performance. Therefore, the core challenge in the TFP domain is: **Can we build a FL framework that protects privacy and commercial secrets, while effectively solving the communication and performance challenges posed by complex models and spatio-temporal heterogeneity?**

In response to all these challenges, the academic community proposed a comprehensive solution based on FL [4]. This solution is a multi-layered, progressive innovation. First, to accurately capture the "temporal" nature of traffic flow, the framework selected the advanced **GRU** neural network as its core prediction model. By embedding GRU into the FL framework, the researchers constructed a **FedGRU algorithm** that combines both privacy preservation and temporal prediction capabilities. Second, to address the **communication overhead** caused by deep learning models, the framework adopted the classic **FedAVG** algorithm. FedAVG, however, can still be overwhelmed when the number of clients (organizations) is too large. Therefore, the study further designed a **"Joint-Announcement Protocol."** This is a clever optimization: in each training round, the cloud server **"randomly subsamples"** only a small fraction (e.g., $\beta = 40\%$) of all organizations to participate in the training and aggregation. This sampling mechanism drastically reduces the communication load per round, significantly enhancing the system's **scalability** in "large-scale" scenarios. Most critically, to solve the **Non-IID data heterogeneity** problem, the study proposed a **"FedGRU scheme based on ensemble clustering."** This scheme recognizes that the heterogeneity of traffic data primarily stems from geographical location. Therefore, before training begins, it first uses a K-Means clustering algorithm to automatically group organizations into K "Clusters" based on their **geographical coordinates** (latitude and longitude). Next, it **trains an independent** FedGRU global model *within each geographical cluster*. Finally, it uses an **"Ensemble Learning"** scheme to combine these K best-performing regional models into a final, high-performance ensemble model. This "cluster first, then federate, then ensemble" strategy perfectly aligns with the "spatio-temporal correlation" physics of traffic flow.

The framework was validated on a **real-world dataset** from the Caltrans Performance Measurement System (PeMS), which contains massive data from over 39,000 detectors. The experimental results were convincing. On the **privacy vs. accuracy** trade-off, the accuracy of the privacy-preserving FedGRU model (RMSE 11.04) was **"very close"** to the non-privacy-preserving centralized GRU model (RMSE 9.97) that required access to all data. This proves the solution achieved "minuscule accuracy degradation" while "privacy was well-preserved." In terms of **scalability**, the **"Joint-Announcement Protocol"** (i.e., large-scale FedGRU) was highly effective. In a setting with 10 clients and a 50% sampling rate ($\beta = 50\%$), the protocol successfully **reduced communication overhead by 64.10%** while maintaining stable model convergence. On **Non-IID performance**, the **"ensemble clustering"** scheme was the most outstanding. By grouping similar organizations geographically (those with similar spatio-temporal features), the scheme not only overcame the Non-IID challenge but actually further improved model performance. When the number of clusters K=10, the RMSE dropped to 9.49. This means that the **privacy-preserving federated model ultimately "outperformed" the non-privacy-preserving centralized GRU model**. This research provides a complete, viable technical blueprint for solving the "data silo" problem in TFP. It clearly demonstrates how to build a system that can (via FedGRU) **protect data privacy and commercial secrets**, (via the Joint-Announcement Protocol) **scale efficiently**, and (via ensemble clustering) intelligently **handle spatio-temporal heterogeneity**. Similar to Case 1, this work again proves that FL is not just a performance "compromise" for privacy—through clever algorithmic design combined with domain knowledge (like geographical clustering), the federated paradigm has the potential to build a more accurate and powerful intelligent system than traditional centralized methods.

4.1.3 Case 3: Intelligent Security Detection with Byzantine-Robust FL

As V2X and edge computing rapidly deploy, ITS are evolving from isolated vehicle intelligence into a fully connected, distributed intelligent network. In this new "FL setting," massive numbers of vehicles, RSUs, and even personal devices (like mobile phones) can act as "worker machines," collectively participating in training. This paradigm holds enormous potential for applications like intelligent scheduling, traffic management, and network security detection (e.g. IDS).

This open, decentralized environment, however, also introduces a fatal **security vulnerability**. Unlike controllable servers in a data center, participants in a V2X network are not inherently trustworthy. The system must assume that a fraction of these "worker machines" may exhibit "Byzantine failures"—that is, they may display "arbitrary and potentially adversarial behavior" due to hardware faults, software crashes, or even malicious attacks (e.g., "zombie cars" or hijacked RSUs). The severity of this problem lies in the fact that FL's standard aggregation algorithm—for example, "naive aggregation," which simply "averages" (mean) all uploaded model updates—is extremely fragile in this environment. Academic research has shown that **even a single Byzantine attacker** can "arbitrarily skew" the final global model by sending a carefully crafted malicious update, leading to a "major degradation in learning performance." If this corrupted global model is a network-wide security IDS or a critical intelligent scheduling model, the consequences would be catastrophic. Therefore, the urgent challenge facing the ITS field is: **Can we design an aggregation algorithm that is mathematically "Byzantine-robust," ensuring the global model's accuracy and optimal statistical performance even when under malicious attack?**

In response to this critical security flaw, academia proposed that the core solution is to **replace the vulnerable "mean" aggregator with "robust statistical estimators."** Foundational research focused on analyzing two robust distributed gradient descent (GD) algorithms [6]: **Coordinate-wise Median** and **Coordinate-wise Trimmed Mean**. The logic of the Coordinate-wise Median algorithm is that the server, upon aggregating, no longer computes the average for *each parameter* (i.e., coordinate) in the model, but instead computes the **"median"** of all updates received for that specific parameter. The Coordinate-wise Trimmed Mean algorithm, on the other hand, first discards the largest and smallest β fraction of values received for *each parameter* (i.e., "trims" them), and then computes the "mean" of only the remaining updates.

The effectiveness of these two methods was clearly validated in adversarial experiments on the standard MNIST dataset. In one experiment (training a logistic regression model) facing a 5% fraction of Byzantine attackers, the standard "mean" aggregator's test accuracy **catastrophically collapsed from 88.0%** (with no attack) **to 76.8%, while** under the exact same attack, the **"median"** aggregator (87.2%) and the **"trimmed mean"** aggregator (86.9%) **almost completely resisted the attack**, maintaining near-optimal performance. This defensive effect was shown to be equally significant on more complex Convolutional Neural Network (CNN) models. The contribution of this research is not just experimental, but also provides mathematical proof that both robust aggregators achieve **"order-optimal statistical error rates."** It also reveals an important trade-off: **"Trimmed Mean"** is statistically superior but requires the deployer to **know or estimate** the attacker fraction α in advance (to set the trim proportion β); the **"Median"** algorithm, while slightly less optimal in its theoretical rate, has the significant advantage of **requiring no prior knowledge** whatsoever about the attackers. This foundational work provides the **critical security guarantee** and viable algorithmic basis necessary for deploying FL in open, untrusted, and adversarial environments like V2X.

4.2 Industrial Practices

In Sect. 4.1, we reviewed the cutting-edge academic research in three core domains of smart mobility: perception, prediction, and security. However, academic viability does not always translate to immediate industrial deployment. Industry, in its pursuit of large-scale commercial rollout, faces far harsher real-world constraints than academia typically considers, such as commercial data governance, the heterogeneity of massive device fleets, strict privacy regulations, and the need for extreme robustness and security.

This section analyzes the practices of industry leaders (Tesla, Baidu, and Huawei) in these corresponding domains. We will observe that the "pain points" or "bottlenecks" in their current advanced systems provide the most compelling use cases for the FL solutions discussed in Sect. 4.1. This analysis, moving from industrial challenge to academic counter-measure, clearly demonstrates how FL, as a key enabling technology, bridges the critical gap between theory and practice.

4.2.1 *Case 1: Tesla "Shadow Mode" Mechanism and Federated Evolution of Perception Systems*

In the development of AD technology, achieving safe, efficient, and sustainable self-evolution of algorithms in real traffic environments is one of the core challenges facing the intelligent vehicle industry. The perception system, as the "eyes" of autonomous vehicles, determines whether a vehicle can accurately recognize road scenarios, predict environmental dynamics, and make reasonable decisions. However, real-world traffic environments are highly dynamic and diverse: road structures, lighting conditions, weather, driving behaviors, and unexpected events form an almost infinite combination. Relying solely on laboratory or closed-course data cannot guarantee model generalization or long-term adaptability on a global scale.

To address this challenge, Tesla proposed the "Shadow Mode" mechanism. The primary motivation is to solve two longstanding problems in AD: first, enabling algorithms to learn from real driving data without compromising safety; second, continuously collecting and utilizing real driving data while avoiding the high cost and inefficiency of manual labeling. The core idea of Shadow Mode [1] is to allow the algorithm to run as an "observer" in real driving, rather than taking control. In other words, under full driver control, the system passively runs in the background, predicting the driver's actions and comparing them with actual behavior, thereby continuously generating feedback samples for model optimization.

This mechanism bridges the gap between "algorithm training" and "real deployment." Vehicles serve as real-time feedback nodes, drivers act as invisible supervisors, and the cloud platform functions as the core of continuous learning. Through this closed loop, the perception model is continuously optimized via dynamic real-world feedback, forming a true "data-to-knowledge-to-model" cycle. Nevertheless, despite the significant improvements, centralized learning still suffers from heavy communication loads, privacy risks, and limited cross-domain generalization.

Shadow Mode constructs a typical vehicle-to-cloud closed-loop learning structure. Onboard vehicles utilize multimodal sensors, including eight cameras, millimeter-wave radar, ultrasonic sensors, and an inertial measurement unit (IMU), to perceive environmental information. The onboard FSD chip provides real-time computing power for local feature extraction and inference. The Shadow Mode model continuously predicts driver actions, such as steering, braking, or accelerating, and calculates deviations between predictions and actual behavior. Events exceeding a predefined threshold are marked as "high-value samples." Only key frames, radar data, and contextual information are cached and uploaded, reducing communication pressure while ensuring coverage of critical samples.

The cloud is responsible for data cleaning, anonymization, and semi-automated labeling, combining human review with model inference to generate training datasets. Cleaned data is sent to perception model pipelines, including object detection, semantic segmentation, trajectory prediction, and scene classification. After training, updates are delivered to vehicles via OTA, ensuring fleet-wide model synchronization. Each update feeds back into the next round of data sampling and deviation detection, forming a closed-loop iterative process that continuously optimizes the perception model in real roads without manual intervention. Despite its efficiency, the centralized architecture still faces computational and storage pressure, cross-border data compliance issues, and adaptation delays in rapidly changing environments.

The core technical foundation of Shadow Mode lies in passive supervised learning and automatic key-sample mining, summarized in a three-stage cycle. First, during normal driving, the background model predicts potential next driver actions and computes deviations from actual behavior. Deviations within thresholds are considered normal, while deviations exceeding thresholds are labeled as learning opportunities. Second, the system automatically records several seconds of multimodal data before and after the event, generates metadata labels, and encrypts uploads to the cloud, forming a collection of real samples representing model weaknesses. Third, the cloud aggregates global key samples, employs incremental training to continuously optimize model parameters, and quickly distributes updates via OTA. Each driving event can become an opportunity for algorithm improvement, forming a large distributed data-driven learning network.

Despite industrial success, Shadow Mode relies on centralized data aggregation and retraining, preventing real-time knowledge sharing between vehicles. Features learned by one vehicle in complex scenarios cannot be immediately transferred to others, and centralized storage increases data exposure risks and privacy concerns. This highlights the need for future AD to adopt distributed, privacy-preserving, and real-time collaborative learning mechanisms.

Experimental results show that global deployment of Shadow Mode significantly improves perception system performance: obstacle detection and scene recognition accuracy increased by approximately 10–15%, and false detection rates decreased by roughly 20%, particularly in low-light, high-glare, and complex intersection scenarios. Additionally, Shadow Mode's data sampling mechanism helped Tesla build the largest real-world driving dataset to date, shortening iteration cycles beyond competitors. However, the centralized mode still suffers from update latency and limited cross-domain generalization, as periodic data uploads and cloud training prevent instantaneous model improvements fleet-wide; variations in regional data distributions also hinder global model adaptation to diverse environments.

The industrial success of Shadow Mode exposes deep technical challenges, including communication and computational pressure, privacy compliance risks, and insufficient cross-domain adaptation and real-time collaboration. With increasing sensor resolution and fleet size, each vehicle can generate tens of gigabytes of perception data daily. Continuous uploading to the cloud would create unsustainable bandwidth and computational demands. Perception data contains sensitive information such as faces, license plates, and geolocation, posing cross-border regulatory compliance risks (e.g., GDPR or China's Data Security Law). Centralized global models also struggle to adapt to regional traffic environments and cannot support instant learning for emergent events.

To address these challenges, Liang et al. proposed a DFL framework (Fig. 4.1) [5], providing an academic evolution path and technical improvement strategy for Shadow Mode. DFL employs a multi-layer vehicle-edge-cloud collaboration mecha-

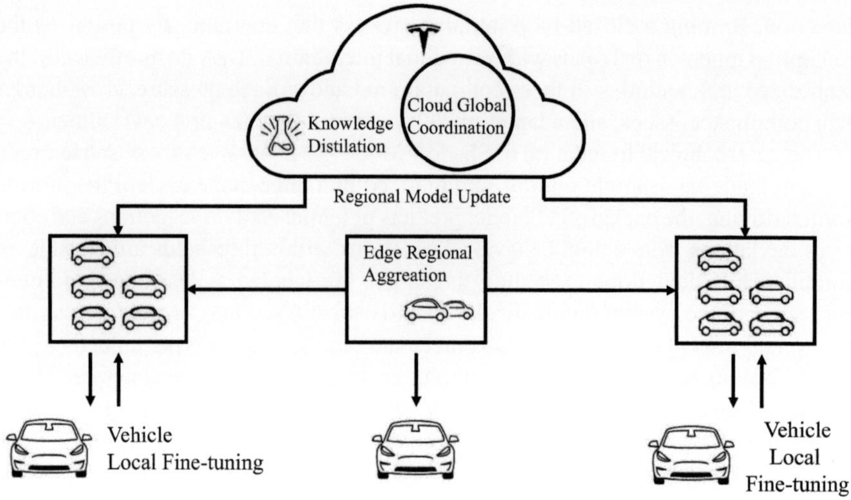

Fig. 4.1 Algorithmic flowchart of the DFL framework combined with Tesla's Shadow Mode mechanism

nism, integrating data privacy protection, distributed intelligence, and dynamic generalization. In the DFL architecture, vehicles perform local model fine-tuning and upload only gradients or weight differences; edge servers aggregate regional vehicle updates to generate specialized regional models; the cloud coordinates cross-region models and knowledge distillation, using dynamic weighted aggregation to ensure global consistency.

Essentially, DFL inherits the core idea of Shadow Mode—real-world feedback for algorithmic self-evolution—but provides a more future-oriented implementation: Shadow Mode relies on centralized data uploads to form a learning loop, whereas DFL constructs a decentralized ecosystem through distributed knowledge collaboration and multi-layer intelligence; the former depends on cloud retraining, while the latter enables autonomous vehicle-edge-cloud co-evolution; the former emphasizes data accumulation, the latter emphasizes knowledge fusion and collaborative evolution.

From an engineering perspective, the federated approach is highly feasible. Modern vehicles are equipped with high-performance chips, 5G-V2X communication, edge computing, and cloud platforms, fully supporting local model training and asynchronous parameter exchange. FL integrates naturally with vehicle-road collaborative systems, allowing regional aggregation and model synchronization via edge nodes, improving real-time adaptability while preserving privacy.

From a macro perspective, Tesla Shadow Mode and its federated evolution illustrate the learning trajectory of intelligent mobility systems: moving from centralized models to distributed collaborative intelligence. FL enables each vehicle to act not only as a data producer but also as a knowledge propagator and learning unit. Through multi-layer collaborative learning across vehicles, roads, and cloud, future

ITS can achieve continuous evolution, privacy protection, and global optimization, shifting AD from single-vehicle algorithm-driven to fleet-wide intelligence-driven, ultimately realizing a truly "smart mobility" ecosystem.

4.2.2 *Case 2: Baidu Apollo Platform and Heterogeneous Data Prediction*

In urban traffic systems, tasks such as vehicle perception, TFP, and route planning are highly dependent on data. Significant differences exist in data types, formats, and distributions across regions, manufacturers, and infrastructures. For example, the sensor suite of vehicles from one manufacturer may include multiple cameras, millimeter-wave radars, and ultrasonic detectors, while another manufacturer may use a different combination; RSUs in different cities vary in deployment locations, data upload frequency, and network latency; government traffic management authorities hold macroscopic vehicle flow statistics, event detection, and high-definition map data, which are both commercially sensitive and privacy-critical. This multidimensional heterogeneity (Non-IID data distribution), data silos (each party reluctant to share raw sensitive data), and competitive relationships among participants render traditional centralized models impractical. For instance, if an OEM uploads detailed vehicle sensor data to a central server, it may expose commercial advantages or technical details; if infrastructure providers or governmental agencies open their geolocation or traffic monitoring data, privacy or security regulations may be violated. In such heterogeneous and distributed data environments, the generalization ability of centralized models is often limited. Therefore, the core motivation of the Apollo platform is to enable multi-party collaborative intelligence while maintaining local data autonomy and security, constructing traffic intelligence models that are generalizable and capable of real-time updates, and transforming isolated data silos into shared knowledge.

To address these challenges, the Apollo platform [2] establishes a three-layer Vehicle-Edge-Cloud (V-E-C) collaborative architecture. The vehicle layer is responsible for frontline data acquisition and preliminary computation; each vehicle is equipped with multimodal sensors (cameras, radar, IMU, GNSS, etc.) capable of local feature extraction and model fine-tuning, identifying key events and uploading encrypted parameters or weight differentials to ensure privacy and optimize bandwidth. The edge layer, deployed at regional traffic hubs or RSUs, aggregates regional models, performs local filtering and optimization, and uploads necessary updates to the cloud to reduce vehicle-to-cloud communication pressure while generating differentiated regional models. The cloud serves as a global coordination center, integrating vehicle and edge models through knowledge distillation, performing dynamic weighted aggregation, and deploying updated models via OTA to vehicles and edge nodes to maintain global model consistency and real-time updates. This architecture allows Apollo to ensure local data processing while achieving cross-domain collaborative training and knowledge sharing.

At the core mechanism level, the Apollo platform implements privacy-preserving and data-minimization techniques: raw data remains local, while only encrypted parameters or weight differentials are uploaded; SecAgg and DP methods prevent information leakage, and communication compression and encoding reduce upload load. Multimodal collaborative distillation enables the edge layer to fuse visual, radar, pose, and time-series signals into comprehensive features, with modality alignment reducing performance loss across different sensors. A hierarchical dynamic aggregation strategy clusters nearby vehicles or RSUs, performs asynchronous aggregation at the edge, and then uploads regional models to the cloud for cross-region integration, dynamically adjusting aggregation weights to prioritize high-quality nodes. The system also supports automatic key-event labeling, compressing and uploading extreme scenario samples to enhance training, improving the model's ability to predict rare events.

In terms of experimental results, existing Apollo cases demonstrate that local vehicle training and edge aggregation can accurately predict traffic flows in specific regions. In a simulated urban network environment, vehicle-level models can quickly identify and respond to congestion, anomalous obstacles, and adverse weather events. Edge-aggregated models improve prediction accuracy by approximately 8–12% within the same region and reduce local misclassification rates. Cloud-based knowledge distillation and dynamic weighting further enhance cross-region generalization, particularly in mixed-fleet scenarios with vehicles from different manufacturers, reducing average prediction error by 5–7% and effectively addressing non-IID data distribution. However, limitations remain: inter-region model adaptability is insufficient, prediction accuracy drops significantly in areas with extreme weather or frequent traffic anomalies, communication load remains high in dense fleets, privacy and regulatory compliance require further assurance, and system real-time responsiveness still experiences latency under sudden events.

To address these limitations, the FedGRU model proposed in *Privacy-Preserving TFP: A FL Approach* Liu et al. [4] provides a feasible solution path. FedGRU is built upon GRUs for processing traffic flow time-series data, with each client training on its own historical data to predict future traffic states. Its gated architecture captures long-term dependencies, mitigating gradient vanishing issues. Local training ensures raw data remains on vehicles or RSUs, with clients uploading only weight or gradient differentials to preserve privacy. Asynchronous updates and gradient accumulation mechanisms allow the global model to update smoothly despite network latency or computational heterogeneity. SecAgg with encryption and key-sharing ensures that the server cannot access individual client updates, and joint verification protocols prevent malicious tampering. Communication optimization techniques, including gradient compression, sparse updates, and encoding, reduce upload volume to approximately 10% of raw data, effectively alleviating 5G-V2X network bandwidth pressure.

For hierarchical clustering and ensemble strategies, FedGRU divides clients into subgroups based on geographic location, traffic characteristics, or data volume; local models are aggregated within subgroups using FedAvg, and the cloud then integrates global models via distillation or weighted fusion. Dynamic weight allocation optimizes aggregation weights based on sample size, data quality, training accuracy, and communication latency, making the global model more sensitive to scarce scenarios or key regions. For multimodal data, feature alignment maps outputs from different sensors to a shared semantic space, mitigating non-IID performance loss. The cloud model can also quickly incorporate new scenarios, enabling online adaptation to sudden events or extreme weather.

In engineering practice, the FedGRU implementation within the Apollo platform operates across three layers (Fig. 4.2): vehicles run local GRU models using historical traffic and sensor data, uploading only differential weights; edge nodes aggregate models for vehicles of the same city, manufacturer, or RSU type to produce specialized regional models; the cloud executes cross-cluster integration and knowledge distillation to generate global predictive models, which are deployed via OTA to vehicles and edge nodes, ensuring fleet-wide synchronization. Through asynchronous uploads and differential gradient aggregation, the system can update the global model within minutes, providing rapid response to sudden traffic events while balancing real-time performance and generalization.

From a feasibility perspective, modern vehicles are equipped with high-performance computing chips, 5G/C-V2X communication, and V2I systems, providing the hardware and network support for local training, edge aggregation, and cloud collaborative updates. FL frameworks like FedGRU offer a privacy-preserving solution in which "data never leaves the vehicle or manufacturer" while simulta-

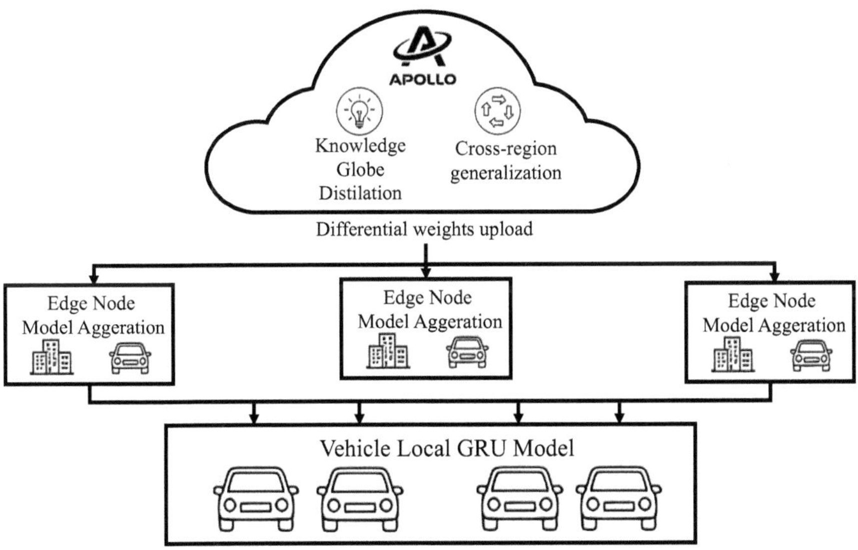

Fig. 4.2 Flowchart of the FedGRU implementation within the Baidu Apollo platform, illustrating the three-layer (V-E-C) operation

neously optimizing models and reducing communication load, addressing the generalization challenges caused by non-IID data. From a macro-level smart mobility perspective, such approaches are significant: in scenarios with multiple stakeholders, heterogeneous and sensitive data, the Apollo platform combined with FL ensures that each vehicle serves not only as a data producer but also as a knowledge-sharing node. Through the three-layer vehicle-edge-cloud collaboration, multimodal fusion, hierarchical dynamic aggregation, and dynamic weight optimization, future intelligent traffic systems can achieve continuous evolution, privacy protection, and global optimization, advancing from a "single-vehicle algorithm-driven" to a "collective intelligence-driven" smart mobility era.

4.2.3 Case 3: Huawei V2X Security and Byzantine-Robust Detection

With the rapid development of ITS and V2X technologies, real-time communication between vehicles and between vehicles and infrastructure has become increasingly complex and critical. Vehicles not only need to share position, speed, and acceleration information but also exchange environment perception data to support AD and coordinated traffic decision-making. In such highly open and dynamically changing environments, ITS faces unprecedented security and robustness challenges. The openness of V2X communication networks allows malicious or compromised nodes to join the network easily, potentially disrupting global decision-making through data injection or model updates. Traditional centralized security strategies, due to communication latency, computational overhead, and insufficient real-time anomaly detection, struggle to ensure system reliability and safety under complex traffic conditions. To address these challenges, Huawei Kaska et al. [3] proposed the V2X-Edge solution, aiming to build a distributed security and Byzantine-robust detection framework centered on edge intelligence. By leveraging multi-layer collaboration among vehicles, RSUs, and the cloud, V2X-Edge enables real-time anomaly detection, distributed collaborative learning, and global model optimization.

The Huawei V2X-Edge architecture adopts a Vehicle-to-Edge (V2E) model, offloading intelligent computation and model deployment to RSUs while combining high-performance on-board computation and 5G-V2X communication to achieve low-latency, real-time security assurance. Vehicles serve as FL clients, collecting environmental and communication data through on-board sensors and communication modules, performing local training and fine-tuning, and uploading only gradient differentials or weight updates rather than raw data streams, thereby reducing bandwidth consumption and protecting privacy. RSUs perform edge aggregation and local anomaly detection. Byzantine-robust aggregation algorithms, such as coordinate-wise median aggregation, process model updates from multiple vehicles to resist the influence of single or a few malicious nodes. Each parameter dimension is statistically analyzed to calculate median values and isolate extreme deviations, ensuring local model stability and security. Lightweight real-time anomaly detection models deployed at RSUs analyze communication packets, message frequency, and behavioral patterns to promptly identify potential attacks, isolate anomalous nodes, and prevent interference with subsequent aggregation. The cloud platform coordinates cross-region models, performs knowledge distillation, and distributes global strategies, ensuring consistency among regional models and OTA-based network-wide synchronization.

Technically, the core innovation of Huawei V2X-Edge lies in its distributed Byzantine-robust FL framework, which maintains high accuracy and security in adversarial environments. Multi-layer collaboration is dynamically adaptive: vehicles conduct local training and fine-tuning, edge RSUs aggregate regional models, and the cloud performs cross-region knowledge distillation to generate a global model optimizing network performance across regions. Compared with traditional centralized training, this multi-layer asynchronous approach reduces communication pressure while ensuring global model stability in the presence of node failures or malicious attacks. Additionally, V2X-Edge employs asynchronous parameter updates so that delayed nodes do not compromise overall robustness, while effectively handling non-IID data across vehicles and regions, thereby improving model generalization and adaptability. Each vehicle thus acts not only as a data collector but also as a knowledge propagator, participating in global model iteration and optimization to form a distributed self-evolving intelligence loop.

Experimental results show that Huawei V2X-Edge exhibits significant performance advantages under large-scale deployment. In scenarios simulating single-point and multi-point malicious node attacks, global model accuracy using Byzantine-robust aggregation remains above 95%, whereas conventional FedAvg mean aggregation shows substantial performance degradation under similar conditions. The system can detect anomalies caused by GPS spoofing or message injection attacks in real-time, with average detection latency below 50 ms, meeting ITS requirements for real-time performance and safety. Gradient differentials and encrypted parameter transmission reduce communication overhead by approximately 60% while maintaining key parameter coverage. Large-scale deployment tests demonstrate system stability even with 100+ RSUs and 5000+ vehicles, illustrating scalability and engineering feasibility.

Despite these achievements, challenges remain. Due to dynamic node participation and potential malicious or abnormal nodes, edge aggregation may be strongly affected by anomalous updates, potentially biasing or invalidating the global model. High-density node synchronization and edge computation place substantial demands on computation and communication resources, especially in areas with limited network coverage or bandwidth. Furthermore, the non-IID nature of local models during cross-region asynchronous aggregation and knowledge distillation can reduce global consistency, affecting the accuracy of security detection. Gradient differentials and encrypted parameter transmission mitigate privacy risks but cross-border data transfer regulations and compliance issues remain.

To address these limitations, academic research has proposed Byzantine-Robust Distributed Learning (BRDL) methods [6], providing a clear pathway for academic evolution and technical optimization of Huawei V2X-Edge. BRDL replaces simple averaging (FedAvg) with statistically robust estimators, such as coordinate-wise median or trimmed-mean, ensuring that the global model remains near-optimal even in the presence of a few malicious nodes. Specifically, each vehicle locally computes gradient or weight updates and submits them to the RSU. The RSU computes median or trimmed-mean values for each parameter dimension, isolating outliers to form a robust regional aggregation model. The cloud then integrates these robust regional results via cross-region coordination and knowledge distillation to generate a global model. BRDL provides theoretical guarantees against Byzantine attacks while achieving near-optimal statistical convergence and global performance, ensuring system stability under adversarial conditions.

From an engineering perspective, BRDL is highly compatible with the Huawei V2X-Edge edge architecture (Fig. 4.3). Vehicles continue local fine-tuning, uploading only encrypted parameters or gradient differentials; edge RSUs implement robust aggregation, and the cloud performs cross-region integration and global model coordination. This multi-layer robust collaboration allows the system to effectively resist a small number of malicious nodes while preserving data privacy, enabling unified real-time security detection, distributed learning, and adaptive intelligence. BRDL's asynchronous update and parameter correction strategies allow non-IID data from heterogeneous vehicles to be effectively integrated, enhancing global model generalization and cross-region adaptability. Each vehicle behavior record and anomalous event can contribute to model optimization, forming a continuous iterative, robust self-evolving learning loop.

From a macro perspective, integrating BRDL into Huawei V2X-Edge demonstrates the evolution of ITS from traditional centralized or simple edge collaboration toward distributed, robust, secure, and real-time intelligent coordination. Vehicles

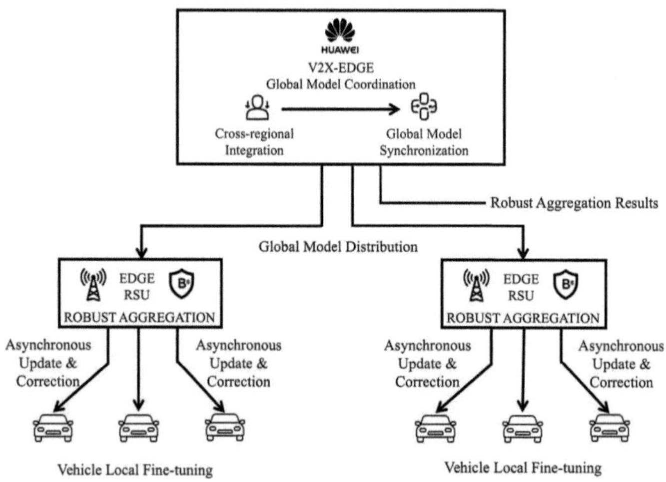

Fig. 4.3 Flowchart of the BRDL mechanism integrated with the Huawei V2X-Edge architecture

act not only as data collection nodes but also as knowledge propagators and model optimization units, while edge and cloud platforms form a multi-layer collaborative ecosystem for global intelligence optimization and security assurance. With the proliferation of 5G/6G networks, edge computing, and high-performance onboard platforms, Huawei V2X-Edge combined with BRDL is expected to achieve true Byzantine robustness, real-time intelligent decision-making, and global optimal coordination in open environments, providing a solid technical foundation for future smart transportation systems.

4.3 Comparative Analysis

The previous two sections provided an in-depth exploration of FL in academic research (Sect. 4.1) and industrial practice (Sect. 4.2), revealing significant divergences between theoretical "optimal solutions" and "viable solutions" for large-scale deployment. This section synthesizes these two perspectives by conducting a comprehensive comparison across four core dimensions—performance, scalability, privacy & security, and deployment cost—to distill key lessons learned and identify critical directions for future research (Fig. 4.4). Table 4.1 provides a high-level summary of the key differences in priorities between the two domains.

On **performance metrics**, the two sides exhibit a fundamental misalignment of priorities. Academic research is primarily driven by "model-centric" metrics: the goal is to achieve state-of-the-art model accuracy (e.g., lower RMSE or higher mAP) and faster theoretical convergence. The academic cases (like 4.1.1 and 4.1.2) made

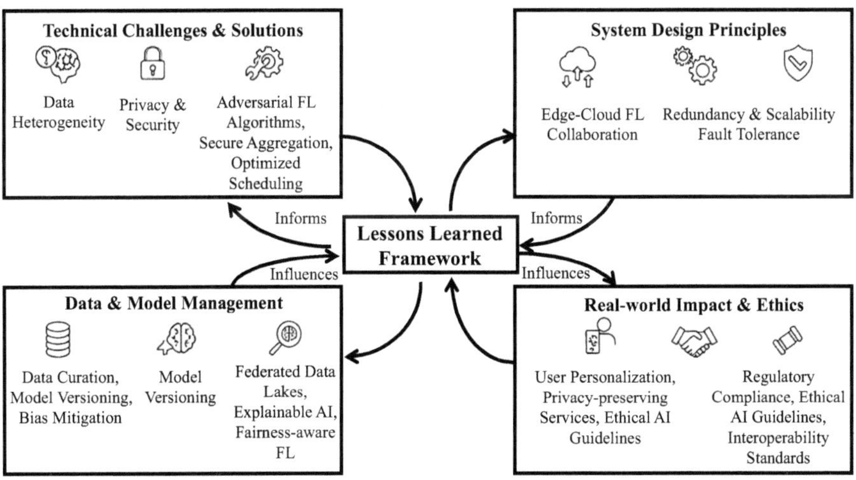

Fig. 4.4 A framework summarizing the key lessons learned from the comparison of academic research and industrial practice

Table 4.1 Comparison of core metrics in academic research versus industrial practice

Metric	Academic research (Sect. 4.1)	Industrial practice (Sect. 4.2)
Core performance metric	**Model-Centric**: Focuses on optimal model accuracy (e.g., RMSE, mAP) and theoretical convergence speed	**System-Centric**: Prioritizes system viability, such as inference latency, power consumption, and robustness
Communication/Learning strategy	**Iterative and frequent**: Tends toward algorithms with many (e.g., hundreds or thousands of) synchronous or asynchronous training rounds	**Pragmatic and infrequent**: Prefers event-triggered, offline batch updates, such as "Shadow Mode"
Privacy and security	**Strong and formal**: Focuses on mathematically provable guarantees (e.g., Byzantine-Robustness, Differential Privacy)	**Pragmatic and balanced**: Uses anonymization and, if necessary, uploads targeted raw data snippets to ensure model performance
Deployment and cost	**Algorithmic and theoretical**: Cost is primarily measured in algorithmic complexity and communication rounds	**Physical and compliance-based**: Cost is measured in expensive physical infrastructure (e.g., FSD chips, 5G RSUs) and long-term compliance maintenance

a significant contribution by demonstrating that the accuracy of federated models could even "surpass" traditional centralized models. Industrial practice, in contrast, is governed entirely by "system-centric" metrics: Tesla's (4.2.1) core focus is the "inference latency" of its onboard chip, measured in milliseconds; other large-scale applications (like Google's) prioritize minimal impact on the user's "battery life and power consumption" and zero disruption to the user experience. In industry, model robustness and real-time responsiveness are far more important than achieving the absolute highest model accuracy.

On **scalability and system complexity**, the gap between theory and practice is particularly stark. Academic research (like 4.1.1) tends to propose "clean," self-contained architectures, such as fully decentralized P2P networks, and simulates them on a limited number of clients. Industrial deployments, like Baidu's Apollo (4.2.2), must manage "extreme scale and heterogeneity"—connecting vehicles from different manufacturers with different sensors, as well as edge nodes in different cities. This real-world complexity "forces" industry to adopt complex "hybrid architectures," such as the "V-E-C" three-tier collaborative system, which uses hierarchical aggregation to manage local intelligence and reduce cloud overhead.

On **privacy and security strength**, a clear line is drawn between the "ideal" and the "practical." Academic research (like 4.1.3) focuses on exploring "strong security" guarantees with mathematical proofs, such as Byzantine-robustness capable of defending against an α fraction of attackers, or the formal protection offered by ϵ-DP. Industry, however, has found in practice that the "utility cost" (i.e., model accuracy degradation) of strong privacy techniques like DP is often "unacceptably" high, especially in safety-critical applications. Consequently, industry universally adopts a "pragmatic, balanced" approach: for example, Tesla (4.2.1) relies on data anonymization and the targeted upload of "raw sensor data snippets" rather than pure FL. This approach satisfies their commercial and legal needs without compromising model performance.

Finally, on **deployment and maintenance costs**, the considerations are also entirely different. An academic study's cost is primarily measured in "algorithmic complexity" and "communication rounds." Industrial practice, however, faces "massive physical infrastructure investment." Tesla's model (4.2.1) depends on its powerful private cloud and the FSD chip being standard in all its vehicles. The V-E-C architectures of Baidu (4.2.2) and Huawei (4.2.3) are predicated on the "large-scale rollout" of expensive 5G and RSU edge servers. Furthermore, industry must bear the high "compliance costs" and "long-term system maintenance costs" that are typically ignored in academic simulations.

Synthesizing these comparisons, we can distill several key "Lessons Learned" across three levels:

At the technical level, first, model and system design must "co-evolve." Case 4.1.1 (FADNet) and 4.2.1 (Tesla FSD chip) jointly demonstrate that the success of FL (or its variants) depends not only on the algorithm but also on specialized hardware and network architectures to handle Non-IID data and performance bottlenecks. Second, "robustness is a prerequisite for collaborative intelligence." Cases 4.1.3 and 4.2.3 (Huawei) clearly show that in an open V2X environment, using a robust aggregator like "coordinate-wise median" to replace "naive mean" is a necessary condition for deploying a secure IDS, not an option.

At the practical level, the most critical lesson is that in the current industrial phase (especially in safety-critical domains), the primary application of FL is **not real-time online learning, but rather an "offline model optimization loop."** Academic research often simulates thousands of rounds of "frequent communication," whereas Tesla's "Shadow Mode" (4.2.1) is the quintessential industrial practice: it is an asynchronous, infrequent "federated data-sourcing loop" triggered by specific events (like driver intervention). This pragmatic deployment model massively reduces communication costs and system interference.

At the administrative level, FL is not just a technical tool, but a **management tool for solving "data governance" and "commercial trust."** Baidu's case (4.2.2) is particularly salient; the core value of its V-E-C open platform is to provide a neutral framework. FL is the only viable path that allows mutually competing OEMs, governments, and infrastructure providers to collaborate while keeping "data within their domains." This highlights that "inter-agency collaboration" is the largest bottleneck, and **"standardization" is the only way forward**. Without uniform data formats, APIs, and security protocols, neither Baidu's V-E-C architecture nor Huawei's V2X-Edge (4.2.3) ecosystem can ever achieve true interoperability.

These identified key gaps between performance, scalability, security, and cost, along with the lessons learned from industrial practice, clearly point to the directions where future research is needed. The bottlenecks revealed by industry (Sect. 4.2)—stemming from massive heterogeneous devices, complex system architectures, and commercial trust barriers—are precisely the challenges that academic research (Sect. 4.1) is attempting to solve.

Summary

This chapter has provided an in-depth exploration of FL in the context of smart mobility, connecting cutting-edge academic breakthroughs with large-scale industrial deployments through a series of key case studies. The chapter's core findings reveal the evolutionary path of FL in addressing the three central challenges of intelligent transportation—perception, prediction, and security—while also exposing the critical gaps between theoretical ideals and real-world bottlenecks.

At the **academic technical breakthrough** level (Sect. 4.1), we saw a series of elegant solutions targeting the specific hard problems of smart mobility. Research demonstrated that through specialized architectures (like FADNet) and fully decentralized topologies (P2P DFL), VFL can not only solve the Non-IID data challenge but also has the potential for its performance to "surpass" traditional centralized methods. In TFP, the FedGRU scheme, by incorporating domain knowledge (like geographical clustering), was also proven to intelligently handle spatio-temporal heterogeneity and achieve accuracy comparable to, or even better than, centralized models, all while preserving privacy. In security, academia provided mathematically provable "Byzantine-robust" aggregators (like coordinate-wise median), solving the trust crisis in open networks at an algorithmic level.

At the **practical industrial experience** level (Sect. 4.2), we observed a distinctly different evolutionary model, one driven by real-world "pain points." Tesla's "Shadow Mode" (4.2.1) showcased a pragmatic "federated data-sourcing loop" that prioritizes data collection efficiency and cost over implementing a pure FL system. Baidu's Apollo platform (4.2.2) treats FL as a "commercial and governance tool," where the core value of its V-E-C architecture is to solve the "data silo" and "commercial trust" problems among competing partners (OEMs, government). Huawei's V2X-Edge solution (4.2.3) highlighted the necessity of robustness—in an open, adversarial environment, Byzantine robustness is a "necessary prerequisite" for deploying a distributed security system (like an IDS), not an option.

The chapter's **Key Gaps and Future Trends** (Sect. 4.3) were clarified in the comparison. Academia pursues "model optimality" (high accuracy, strong privacy), whereas industry pursues "system viability" (low latency, low power consumption, manageable costs, and compliance-first). This gap has led to a key current trend: the application of FL in safety-critical domains is primarily an "offline optimization" mechanism (like Tesla's asynchronous loop) rather than high-frequency "real-time online learning." Furthermore, industrial practice has revealed that the success of FL is heavily dependent on expensive physical infrastructure (like FSD chips and 5G RSUs) and complex hybrid system architectures (V-E-C).

In summary, this chapter has clearly outlined the current state of FL in smart mobility: it has evolved from a theoretical concept into a key enabling technology for solving the industry's core bottlenecks (privacy compliance, data silos, and open-network security). However, the explorations of both academia and industry jointly point to a series of pressing challenges that remain to be solved. These challenges—stemming from massive heterogeneous devices, complex system architectures, high deployment costs, and commercial trust barriers—have not yet been perfectly resolved. These remaining challenges in performance, scalability, security, and governance are precisely the core topics that the next chapter of this book, "Challenges and Future Directions," will explore in depth.

References

1. Aswathnarayana, S.: How tesla has been optimizing its software and hardware for fsd capabilities and a hyper efficient robo-taxi fleet? Towards AI (2023). https://towardsai.net/p/l/how-tesla-has-been-optimizing-its-software-and-hardware-for-fsd-capabilities-and-a-hyper-efficient-robo-taxi-fleet
2. Fan, H., Zhu, F., Liu, C., Zhang, L., Zhuang, L., Li, D., Zhu, W., Hu, J., Li, H., Kong, Q.: Baidu apollo em motion planner (2018). arXiv:1807.08048
3. Kaska, K., Beckvard, H., Minárik, T.: Huawei, 5g and china as a security threat. In: NATO Cooperative Cyber Defence Center for Excellence (CCDCOE), vol. 28, pp. 1–26 (2019)
4. Liu, Y., James, J., Kang, J., Niyato, D., Zhang, S.: Privacy-preserving traffic flow prediction: a federated learning approach. IEEE Internet Things J. **7**(8), 7751–7763 (2020)
5. Nguyen, A., Do, T., Tran, M., Nguyen, B.X., Duong, C., Phan, T., Tjiputra, E., Tran, Q.D.: Deep federated learning for autonomous driving. In: 2022 IEEE Intelligent Vehicles Symposium (IV), pp. 1824–1830. IEEE (2022)
6. Yin, D., Chen, Y., Kannan, R., Bartlett, P.: Byzantine-robust distributed learning: Towards optimal statistical rates. In: International Conference on Machine Learning, pp. 5650–5659. PMLR (2018)

Chapter 5
Challenges and Future Directions

Abstract This chapter discusses the key technical challenges and future directions in the field of FL for smart mobility. It begins by exploring the technical challenges, including data heterogeneity, communication and bandwidth limitations, model scalability and complexity, security and robustness, and energy consumption, all of which hinder the widespread deployment of FL in transportation systems. The chapter then identifies unresolved pain points and highlights emerging paradigms that may overcome these obstacles, such as the integration of FL with blockchain for trust and auditing, 6G communication for ultra-low latency, and edge intelligence for resource-adaptive FL. The concept of digital twins for virtual-physical system integration is discussed as a potential breakthrough for modeling and simulation. Additionally, the chapter introduces large models and adaptive FL approaches that aim to address the challenges of scalability and resource limitations. It also emphasizes the importance of policy, ethics, and standardization, discussing compliance frameworks, algorithm transparency, fairness, and accountability in the context of FL applications. Finally, the chapter offers a vision for sustainable and secure transportation systems, outlining pathways to realize this vision while connecting the themes discussed throughout the book.

Keywords FL · Technical challenges · Data heterogeneity · Communication limitations · Scalability · Security · Blockchain · 6G · Edge intelligence · Digital twin · Adaptive FL · Policy · Ethics · Standardization · Sustainable mobility

5.1 Technical Challenges

The deployment of FL in ITS faces a variety of technical challenges that need to be addressed [30] for the systems to function efficiently. These challenges stem from both the inherent complexities of FL itself and the unique characteristics of ITS. In this section, we summarize the key technical bottlenecks faced by FL in ITS, covering the following major challenges: data heterogeneity, communication and bandwidth limitations, model scalability and complexity, security and robustness, and energy consumption and limited computational resources (Fig. 5.1).

© The Author(s), under exclusive license to Springer Nature Singapore Pte Ltd. 2026
J. Pei et al., *Federated Learning for Smart Mobility*, SpringerBriefs in Computer Science,
https://doi.org/10.1007/978-981-95-6160-5_5

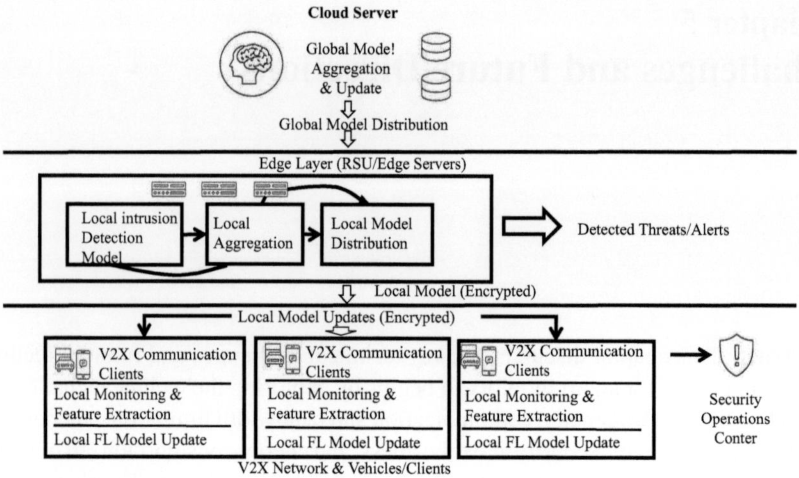

Fig. 5.1 A taxonomy of the major technical challenges for FL in ITS

Data Heterogeneity (Non-IID Data Distribution)

Data heterogeneity, or non-IID) data [28], is one of the most significant challenges in FL for ITS. In federated systems, data across different participants can be diverse in terms of feature distribution, data quality, and collection conditions. For example, vehicles from different manufacturers or regions may collect varying types of sensor data, including different sensor modalities (e.g., radar, LIDAR, cameras), which makes it difficult to aggregate this data for joint model training.

Causes and Impact: The data collected from different entities is often skewed and non-uniform, leading to poor model convergence. Non-IID data can cause federated models to fail to generalize effectively, as each participant's local model may be trained on data that is not representative of the overall population, leading to biases or poor generalization to unseen data.

Existing Solutions and Limitations: To address these challenges, techniques like data augmentation and algorithms such as FedProx (Federated Proximal) [29] have been proposed. FedProx introduces a regularization term to prevent local models from deviating too much from the global model, thus addressing the issue of data heterogeneity. Personalized Federated Learning (PFL) [15] is another approach where models are tailored to each client's local data, but this increases computational complexity. Despite these approaches, achieving optimal model performance across highly heterogeneous data remains an unsolved challenge.

Communication and Bandwidth Limitations

Communication efficiency is a major bottleneck [7] in FL, particularly in ITS where large numbers of vehicles and infrastructure systems participate in the training process. The frequent need to transmit large model updates between clients and the central server imposes high communication costs, especially in environments where bandwidth is limited, such as in urban areas with high traffic or in remote regions with low connectivity.

Causes and Impact: The communication overhead in FL is mainly driven by the large number of model updates that need to be exchanged between the clients and the server. This results in high bandwidth consumption and increased latency, especially as the number of participating devices grows. In ITS, where real-time decision-making is essential (e.g., for AD), delays caused by communication inefficiencies can severely affect the system's performance.

Existing Solutions and Limitations: Several techniques have been proposed to address communication bottlenecks, including client sampling [27], asynchronous updates [10], and model compression. Client sampling reduces the number of participants involved in each training round, which helps decrease communication costs. Asynchronous updates allow clients to send updates as soon as they finish local training, reducing idle times. Model compression techniques [31], such as quantization and sparsification, reduce the size of the updates, thus lowering communication overhead. However, these techniques come with trade-offs—client sampling may lead to biased updates, and aggressive compression may degrade model accuracy. Moreover, achieving effective real-time communication remains a challenge in large-scale ITS environments.

Model Scalability and Complexity

As FL is applied to larger-scale ITS networks, the complexity and scalability of the models become critical factors in their success. The size and complexity of the model, especially in deep learning-based systems, can grow significantly as more data sources are integrated. This leads to higher computational costs and challenges in deploying the models in resource-constrained environments, such as vehicles with limited processing power.

Causes and Impact: Scalability issues arise when the volume of data and participants increases, making it difficult for central servers and edge devices to manage the computation and storage needs. In ITS, the models must be able to handle vast amounts of sensor data and operate efficiently in real-time, which requires both model optimization and efficient resource allocation. Failure to address scalability can result in increased training time, higher computational costs, and delays in real-time decision-making.

Existing Solutions and Limitations: Techniques like model pruning [18], where unnecessary parameters are removed from the model, and edge computing [46], where computation is offloaded to local devices, have been explored to address scalability. These methods reduce the computational load on central servers and edge devices, respectively. However, model pruning can lead to a loss of model accuracy, and edge computing is limited by the computational capabilities of local devices, which may not be sufficient for complex models.

Security and Robustness

Security and robustness are critical considerations [35] in FL, particularly in ITS, where sensitive data—such as vehicle locations, driving behaviors, and infrastructure conditions—are involved. FL's decentralized nature makes it vulnerable to security attacks such as data poisoning [50], model inversion [34], and adversarial attacks, which can compromise both model accuracy and privacy.

Causes and Impact: Security vulnerabilities arise when malicious participants inject false data or model updates, thereby corrupting the global model. The distributed nature of FL makes it difficult to detect and mitigate such attacks in real-time. Additionally, robustness issues arise when the model fails to generalize well under unexpected conditions, such as adversarial or noisy data.

Existing Solutions and Limitations: Solutions such as SecAgg protocols [16] and DP have been proposed to protect the privacy of individual clients' data and ensure secure model updates. Adversarial training and robustness-enhancing techniques can help improve model stability in the presence of malicious attacks. However, security techniques like DP often come at the cost of model accuracy, and adversarial training increases the complexity and computational cost of training. Moreover, existing security solutions are often not robust enough to handle sophisticated attacks in dynamic environments like ITS.

Energy Consumption and Limited Computational Resources

FL's energy consumption and the computational resource limitations of edge devices present significant challenges, particularly in ITS, where vehicles and other devices often operate on battery power. Continuous communication and the computational demands of training large models can drain the limited energy resources of edge devices, thereby limiting system performance.

Causes and Impact: The frequent communication between clients and central servers, coupled with the high computational demands of deep learning models, results in high energy consumption. This can significantly reduce the operational time of edge devices, such as in vehicles, which are critical in real-time applications like AD. Energy constraints may also prevent the participation of certain devices in the FL process, thus reducing the system's scalability.

Existing Solutions and Limitations: Solutions like energy-aware FL, which adjusts model training based on energy consumption, and the use of edge computing to reduce transmission requirements have been explored. Efficient model design, such as using lightweight neural networks, also helps reduce energy usage. However, these

Table 5.1 Challenges and solutions in FL for ITS

Challenge	Current approach	Limitation
Data heterogeneity	FedProx, PFL	High computational complexity, Limited effectiveness in extreme non-IID cases
Communication	Client sampling, Asynchronous updates, Compression	Potential bias, Model inconsistency, Reduced accuracy with aggressive compression
Model scalability	Model Pruning, Adaptive learning rates, Edge computing	Trade-off between accuracy and complexity, Limited edge device capacity
Security	DP, SecAgg, Adversarial training	Privacy-accuracy trade-off, Increased model complexity
Energy consumption	Energy-aware FL, Edge computing, Efficient models	Potential accuracy sacrifice, Edge device limitations

solutions often trade off model accuracy to save energy, and the effectiveness of edge computing is limited by the capabilities of local devices, which may not be powerful enough to handle complex computations.

Summary of Challenges and Solutions

The Table 5.1 summarizes the key challenges in FL for ITS, along with the current approaches and their limitations:

Unresolved Pain Points

While significant progress has been made in addressing these challenges, several pain points remain. The balance between model accuracy, communication efficiency, and energy consumption is still an ongoing research challenge. Moreover, FL systems need to be more resilient to security threats and better at handling extreme cases of non-IID data. Further innovations are needed to develop more scalable and efficient solutions that meet the growing demands of real-world ITS.

5.2 Integrating FL with Emerging Paradigms

FL has gained significant attention for its ability to enable decentralized ML while maintaining privacy. As technology continues to evolve, there is an increasing trend toward integrating FL with emerging paradigms to address the complex demands of ITS. This integration opens up new opportunities for enhancing the efficiency,

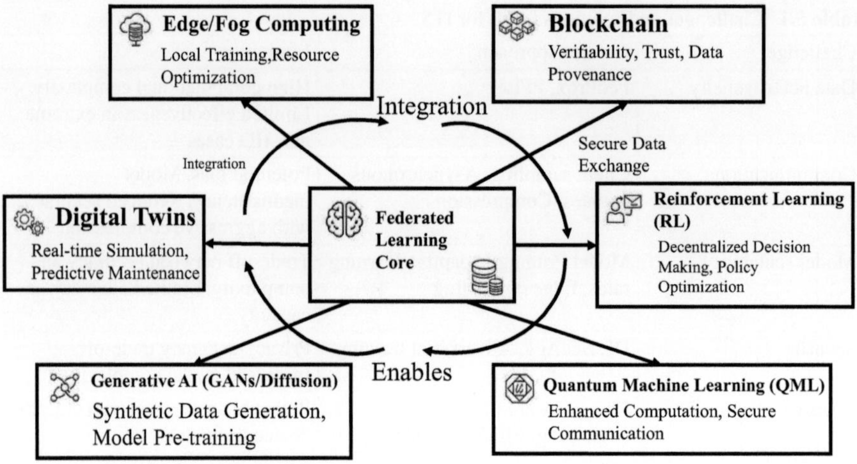

Fig. 5.2 A technology integration map illustrating the fusion of FL with emerging paradigms

security, and scalability of FL systems, while also introducing new challenges. In this section, we explore the integration of FL with five key emerging technologies: Blockchain, 6G communication, Edge Intelligence, Digital Twin, and Large Models with Adaptive FL (LLM-FL/Adaptive FL). These paradigms offer potential breakthroughs in the field of ITS (Fig. 5.2), each bringing unique benefits, as well as their own set of challenges.

Blockchain and FL: Trust and Auditing

Integrating Blockchain with FL offers enhanced trust [39] and transparency through secure and auditable model updates. Blockchain's distributed ledger can provide a secure mechanism for ensuring data integrity and the authenticity of model updates, which is critical in ITS applications where trust is paramount. Blockchain can also serve as a solution for FL's main challenge of validating the correctness of model updates, particularly when multiple participants are involved in training. By maintaining an immutable, transparent record, Blockchain ensures that any malicious or erroneous updates can be easily traced and audited.

Potential Benefits: Blockchain can enhance the security of FL systems by ensuring data authenticity, preventing data tampering, and maintaining trust among all participants. This is especially important in ITS, where data integrity is crucial, such as for AD, traffic prediction models, and other real-time applications.

Challenges: The integration of Blockchain into FL increases computational overhead due to the need for consensus mechanisms, transaction validation, and maintaining the distributed ledger. Moreover, while Blockchain can guarantee trust, managing the privacy of data stored on the Blockchain becomes more complex, especially if public chains are involved. Furthermore, the efficiency of Blockchain integration can be hindered by the high latency and bandwidth requirements inherent in the Blockchain protocol, leading to potential delays in model updates and training.

6G Communication: Ultra-Low Latency and Distributed Intelligence

6G communication promises ultra-low latency, high throughput, and ubiquitous connectivity, which will enable faster, more efficient model updates in real-time ITS applications. The integration of 6G with FL facilitates distributed intelligence, improving the performance and scalability of FL systems by minimizing communication delays and supporting high-speed data transfers. With its high bandwidth and ultra-low latency, 6G communication can significantly enhance the real-time training and deployment of FL models in vehicular networks and smart cities.

Potential Benefits: The integration of FL with 6G communication enables near-instantaneous model updates, reducing the delay between data collection and model training, which is essential for real-time decision-making in ITS. Additionally, the distributed intelligence capabilities of 6G allow for decentralized model training and aggregation, improving the scalability and responsiveness of FL systems. The higher capacity of 6G networks also enables seamless communication between numerous devices (such as vehicles, sensors, and traffic lights) in ITS, thus fostering more efficient model collaboration.

Challenges: Despite the potential of 6G to reduce communication delays, the massive scale of 6G networks introduces challenges related to network management, spectrum allocation, and security. Moreover, as more devices become connected through 6G, ensuring the privacy and confidentiality of data in a highly dynamic and distributed environment becomes more difficult. Additionally, maintaining synchronization and minimizing errors in real-time updates becomes increasingly complex as the number of devices grows.

Edge Intelligence: Resource-Adaptive FL

Edge intelligence refers to the ability of edge devices (such as vehicles, traffic lights, and smart cameras) to process and analyze data locally, without relying heavily on a central server. Integrating FL with edge intelligence can improve the efficiency and responsiveness of FL systems by enabling real-time data processing and decision-making at the edge. By performing local model training and aggregation, edge devices can reduce the communication overhead and latency that typically arise when data is sent to a central server for processing.

Potential Benefits: By processing data locally, edge intelligence reduces the burden on central servers and networks, minimizing the need for high-bandwidth communication. This also enables faster decision-making and model updates, which is particularly important for time-sensitive applications such as AD. Furthermore, integrating FL with edge intelligence ensures that FL models are resource-adaptive, optimizing computational tasks according to the capabilities of local devices.

Challenges: The main challenge in integrating edge intelligence with FL is the limited computational power and storage capacity of edge devices. While edge devices can perform basic computations, they may struggle to handle the full complexity of modern ML models. Furthermore, the integration of distributed edge devices into a FL framework requires robust communication protocols and mechanisms for synchronizing updates across devices.

Digital Twin: Virtual-Physical Integration for Modeling and Simulation

Digital twin technology creates virtual replicas [23] of physical systems, providing real-time simulations that integrate physical and digital data. The integration of FL with digital twins enables the continuous update and optimization of intelligent driving models, improving traffic management, route planning, and AD systems. Digital twins allow for simulations that integrate real-time data from physical environments, such as road conditions, traffic patterns, and vehicle statuses, to generate highly accurate and dynamic models.

Potential Benefits: The integration of FL with digital twins allows for real-time synchronization [42] between physical and virtual systems, providing continuous updates to intelligent driving models. This leads to improved predictive capabilities, real-time optimization, and better-informed decision-making. Additionally, digital twins can simulate a variety of traffic scenarios without the need for physical infrastructure, reducing the costs associated with testing and deployment.

Challenges: One of the main challenges of digital twins is ensuring the accuracy and real-time synchronization of physical and virtual models. If the digital twin does not accurately reflect the real-world system, the FL model may be trained on erroneous data, leading to suboptimal performance. Additionally, continuously updating digital twins requires substantial computational resources, both in terms of processing power and data storage, making it difficult to deploy at scale.

Large Models and Adaptive FL (LLM-FL/Adaptive FL)

The rise of large ML models presents new challenges [6] in FL, particularly in terms of computational demands and communication overhead. Large models, such as deep neural networks, require significant computational resources for training, especially in decentralized settings. Adaptive FL [41], which adjusts the FL process based on the available resources and the characteristics of the data, can help optimize the training of large models in distributed environments.

Potential Benefits: By integrating FL with large models and adaptive learning techniques, it is possible to scale the learning process to handle more complex tasks, such as real-time traffic prediction and AD. Adaptive FL can optimize the FL process by adjusting the frequency of communication, selecting clients based on their resource availability [36], and tailoring model updates according to the system's current state. This ensures that large models can be trained efficiently while maintaining performance.

Challenges: One of the main challenges of integrating large models with FL is the significant computational cost and memory requirements [40]. Large models may require more frequent communication and larger updates, increasing the communication overhead. Additionally, managing the trade-off between model performance and computational efficiency becomes more complex as the size and complexity of the models grow. Adaptive FL aims to address this issue, but it introduces additional complexity in terms of resource management and decision-making.

Summary: Potential Breakthroughs and Challenges

Integrating FL with these emerging paradigms offers tremendous potential for creating more efficient, scalable, and ITS. The key benefits of these integrations include enhanced security, low-latency communication, improved data processing capabilities, and the ability to handle more complex and diverse models. However, these advancements come with significant challenges, including increased energy consumption, higher computational demands, privacy complexities, and difficulties in ensuring real-time synchronization and model accuracy across distributed systems.

The future of FL in ITS will likely depend on how well these emerging paradigms can be integrated and optimized to balance the trade-offs between system performance, energy consumption, and data privacy. As these technologies mature, they could lead to significant breakthroughs in ITS, enabling more responsive, secure, and efficient systems for AD, traffic management, and smart cities.

As shown in Table 5.2, the integration of FL with these emerging paradigms provides both substantial benefits and notable risks, each requiring careful management for successful deployment.

Table 5.2 Integration of FL with emerging paradigms: potential versus risks

Emerging paradigm	Potential benefits	Risks and challenges
Blockchain-FL	Trust and audit trail, Data integrity	Increased computational overhead, Privacy concerns
6G-FL	Ultra-low latency, Real-time updates	Network management complexity, Increased data volume
Edge intelligence	Reduced communication overhead, Real-time processing	Limited device resources, Integration complexity
Digital twin-FL	Accurate modeling, Real-time optimization	High computational demand, Data synchronization challenges
LLM-FL/Adaptive FL	Scalable large model training, Resource adaptation	Increased communication cost, Model complexity

5.3 Policy, Ethics, and Standardization

As ITS and FL evolve, addressing non-technical challenges such as policy, ethics, and standardization becomes paramount [17]. These challenges are deeply intertwined with the systems' societal, legal, and governance frameworks. This section examines key issues related to data governance, privacy compliance [25], algorithm transparency, fairness, and industry standards. Furthermore, it explores the unique constraints faced by ITS, including multi-party involvement [47, 48], cooperation between governments and enterprises, and building public trust (Fig. 5.3).

Compliance and Ethical Frameworks

The integration of FL in ITS requires adherence to complex privacy and data governance regulations, particularly in cross-border data transmission [5]. These regulations aim to safeguard personal information, ensure fair data use, and regulate how organizations handle sensitive information. A key ethical consideration is balancing the benefits of data-driven models with the protection of individual rights.

Data Governance and Cross-Border Data Transfer: The global nature of data sharing in FL presents a significant challenge in ensuring compliance with international regulations. As vehicles, traffic management systems, and infrastructure providers in various regions exchange data, it becomes necessary to implement robust governance practices that adhere to local and international privacy laws. The challenge is further complicated by cross-border data transfer, where data from different jurisdictions may be subject to varying rules and restrictions.

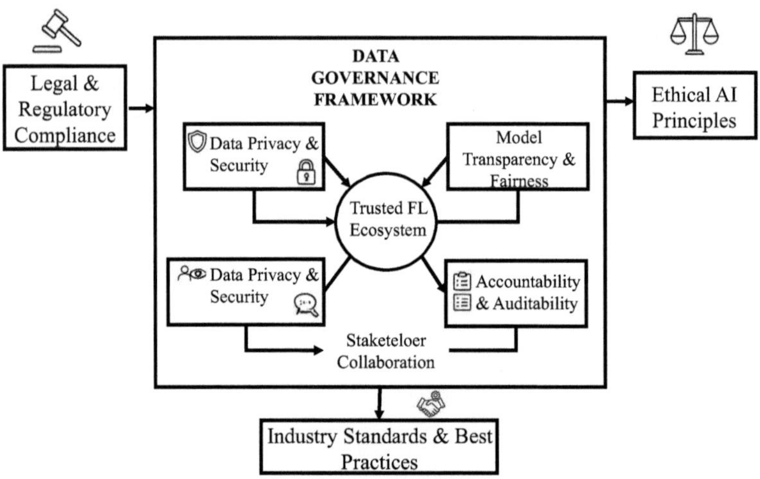

Fig. 5.3 A framework illustrating the relationship between data governance, policy, and ethics in FL

Table 5.3 Comparison of major privacy regulations and compliance requirements

Regulation	Key requirements	Impact on FL
GDPR (EU)	Right to be forgotten, Data minimization, Explicit consent	Requires robust anonymization techniques and explicit user consent
China data security law	Data localization, Cross-border transfer restrictions	Mandates data localization and stringent control over sensitive data
CCPA (California)	Transparency, Data access rights, Opt-out provision	Requires transparency in data collection and model training processes

Privacy Compliance: FL systems, which operate on decentralized data, must navigate complex privacy laws such as the European Union's GDPR [38], China's Data Security Law, and the CCPA [37]. These regulations place stringent requirements on how personal data is collected, stored, and processed. FL enables privacy-preserving data processing by ensuring that raw data never leaves the local device, but privacy challenges remain in terms of model inversion attacks and data leakage through model updates. To comply with these regulations, it is crucial to implement mechanisms that ensure data anonymity and restrict the risk of re-identification.

Table 5.3 compares major privacy regulations, offering an overview of compliance requirements in the context of FL applications in ITS.

Algorithm Transparency and Explainability

As FL is deployed in ITS, it is essential to ensure algorithm transparency and explainability [22]. This is crucial for building trust with stakeholders, including regulators, users, and system developers. While FL provides privacy-preserving advantages, its "black-box" nature raises concerns [44] about how decisions are made, especially in critical systems like AD and traffic management.

Transparency and Accountability: In the context of ITS, transparency involves providing clear and understandable information on how FL models make decisions. This is especially important in safety-critical applications where the consequences of model errors can lead to accidents or system malfunctions. Making these models interpretable ensures accountability and helps regulators evaluate the system's compliance with safety standards.

Ethical Considerations: Along with transparency, the ethical use of algorithms [4] in ITS requires ensuring fairness, accuracy, and non-discrimination. Bias in data collection [33] or model design can perpetuate inequalities, such as creating unfair traffic predictions or biased route recommendations for certain demographic groups. Addressing these concerns requires integrating fairness metrics into the model development and validation processes.

Fairness and Accountability

One of the core challenges in ITS is ensuring fairness [13] in decision-making, particularly when FL models interact with diverse user groups and infrastructures. Fairness involves treating all participants equally, regardless of their background, location, or other demographic factors, and avoiding algorithmic bias.

Fairness in Data Representation: In ITS, fairness concerns often arise from unequal data representation [19]. For instance, if certain geographical regions are underrepresented in training data, FL models might favor decisions that reflect the majority, potentially neglecting minority groups. Achieving fairness in FL requires ensuring diverse and balanced data contributions from all participants in the system, which may require collaboration between public authorities and private organizations.

Responsibility Distribution: Another important ethical challenge is determining responsibility when errors or malfunctions occur. In FL, the responsibility for model performance may be distributed across multiple parties, including data owners, model trainers, and system integrators. Establishing clear guidelines on liability and accountability for system failures is essential to ensure that stakeholders are held responsible in case of mishaps.

Standardization and International Trends

With the rapid development of FL in ITS, standardization has become a critical aspect [53] of ensuring system interoperability, security, and scalability. Establishing industry-wide standards and protocols will facilitate collaboration across different sectors and regions, promoting the broader adoption of FL in transportation systems.

FL Standards: Various international bodies are working on developing standards for FL. Organizations such as IEEE, ISO, and ETSI [11] have already made significant progress in defining the technical specifications for FL systems, including protocols for data sharing, privacy protection, and communication. These standards aim to provide clear guidelines for the design, implementation, and evaluation of FL systems in ITS applications.

Collaboration Between Government and Industry [9]: To ensure that FL systems in ITS are both effective and compliant, it is crucial for governments, private enterprises, and standardization bodies to collaborate closely. Governments must ensure that regulations align with technological advancements, while industries should work within regulatory frameworks to deploy secure and efficient systems. Public-private partnerships [24] will be essential for overcoming the challenges of data sharing, model validation, and trust-building.

Summary: Coordinating Policy, Ethics, and Technology

In conclusion, the integration of FL with ITS presents both opportunities and challenges. On the policy and ethics side, ensuring privacy compliance, algorithm transparency, and fairness is critical for maintaining public trust. Simultaneously, standardization efforts from international bodies are essential for enabling the broad deployment of FL technologies. The collaboration between governments, industries, and standardization bodies will be key to addressing these challenges and ensuring that FL can be deployed responsibly and effectively in ITS. As the technology matures, these policy, ethical, and standardization issues must be addressed to ensure that FL contributes to safer, more efficient, and more equitable transportation systems worldwide.

5.4 Vision for Sustainable and Secure Transportation Systems

As ITS continue to evolve, the vision for the future encompasses a seamless integration of privacy, security, and sustainability, all working together to create a safer, more efficient, and more environmentally-friendly transportation ecosystem (Fig. 5.4). This section outlines a holistic vision for the future of transportation [14], emphasizing the need for synergistic cooperation between technological advancements, social

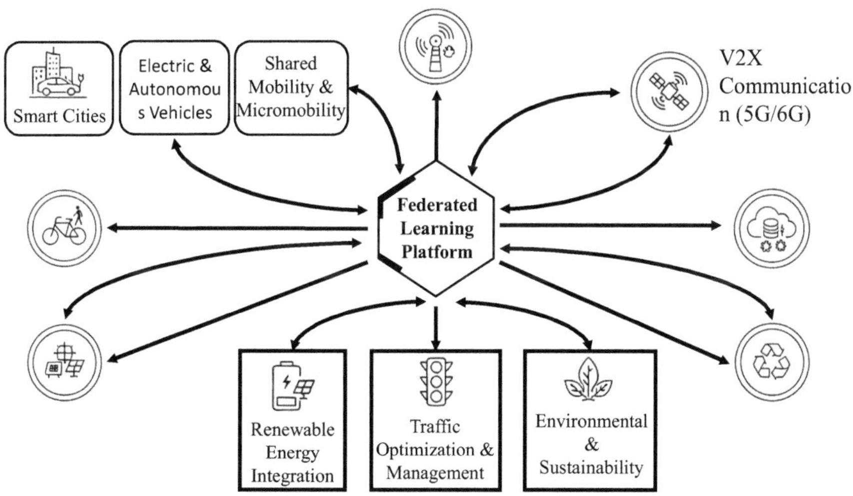

Fig. 5.4 A conceptual diagram of the future vision for a sustainable and secure smart mobility system

responsibility, and policy frameworks. The goal is to build transportation systems that are not only secure and efficient but also sustainable, transparent, and resilient in the face of future challenges.

Blueprint for the Future System

The future transportation system will be underpinned by a comprehensive framework that ensures the coexistence of privacy, security, and sustainability. The vision for these systems can be outlined through the following key objectives:

1. Privacy, Security, and Sustainability Synergy [54]: Privacy and security concerns have always been central to the development of ITS, but as the scale and complexity of these systems grow, it is essential to ensure that privacy, security, and sustainability are not treated as isolated objectives. Instead, they should work together as an integrated framework that supports and enhances one another. For example, secure and privacy-preserving FL models in ITS can contribute to both environmental sustainability by optimizing traffic management (thus reducing emissions) and public trust by ensuring data privacy.

2. The Goal of Zero Emissions [45], **Zero Accidents** [2], **and Zero Trust Gaps** [26]: The ultimate ambition for the future of transportation is to create a system with zero emissions, zero accidents, and zero trust gaps. Zero emissions can be achieved through the widespread adoption of EVs and energy-efficient transportation solutions, while zero accidents can be pursued by enhancing vehicle safety with AI-powered AD and advanced traffic management systems. Furthermore, the concept of zero trust gaps will be realized by ensuring that all stakeholders in the system—whether they be vehicles, infrastructure, or data providers—operate under secure, privacy-preserving, and transparent protocols.

3. Self-organizing, Self-optimizing Transportation Learning Systems [12]: The future system will not only be smart but also self-organizing and self-optimizing, able to adapt to changing conditions in real-time. By integrating FL models, transportation systems will become capable of autonomous data processing and decision-making, minimizing human intervention and maximizing efficiency. These systems will continuously learn from incoming data to improve traffic flow, reduce congestion, and provide real-time updates to all participants, all while respecting privacy constraints.

4. Multi-layered Collaboration between Society, Technology, and Policy [20]: Achieving this vision will require more than just technological advancements. It will need a multi-layered approach involving societal cooperation, technological development, and policy frameworks. Governments, businesses, and individuals must collaborate to ensure that ITS remain both equitable and secure. Social acceptance, trust, and regulatory compliance will be key to ensuring the success and sustainability of these systems.

Pathways to Realizing the Vision

While the vision for a sustainable and secure transportation system is compelling, achieving it will require overcoming significant technical, social, and policy challenges. The following pathways highlight how we can move toward this future:

1. Advancing Privacy-Preserving ML [1] **and Data Sharing**: To realize privacy, security, and sustainability, FL will play a pivotal role in enabling distributed training without compromising privacy. This decentralized approach will ensure that sensitive data, such as vehicle location or driver behavior, never leaves local devices, preserving individual privacy. By combining FL with secure multiparty computation [52] and HE [21], we can further enhance data privacy while optimizing traffic and transportation systems. Furthermore, standardized protocols for privacy-preserving data sharing will be crucial in facilitating cross-border and cross-sector collaboration, paving the way for a truly global ITS infrastructure.

2. Leveraging Advanced Communication Technologies (6G [49], **Blockchain)**: The deployment of 6G networks and blockchain technologies will be key to the success of this vision. 6G's ultra-low latency and high bandwidth will enable near-instantaneous communication between vehicles, infrastructure, and traffic management systems. Blockchain will provide the trust framework needed for secure transactions, model updates, and data sharing. Together, these technologies will lay the foundation for seamless, real-time, and secure communication, ensuring that transportation systems operate with minimal delays and high accuracy.

3. Smart Regulation and Policy Frameworks [32]: Policy makers will need to establish clear and coherent regulatory frameworks that foster innovation while ensuring safety, fairness, and privacy. This includes creating standards for data sharing, defining the responsibilities of different stakeholders in the ecosystem, and ensuring compliance with data protection regulations like GDPR [51], CCPA, and China's Data Security Law. Moreover, governments will play a critical role in incentivizing the transition to green energy, facilitating the adoption of EVs, and promoting sustainable urban mobility practices. Policy frameworks will also need to address issues such as cybersecurity, liability, and accountability [8] in autonomous vehicle systems.

4. Promoting Public-Private Partnerships and Societal Engagement [43]: Achieving a secure and sustainable transportation system will require active collaboration between public authorities, private enterprises, and civil society. Public-private partnerships will be critical in developing the infrastructure and technologies needed to support the transition to smart, sustainable transportation. Engaging the public and raising awareness of the benefits of privacy-preserving, secure, and sustainable systems will be crucial for fostering societal trust. This can include educating users about data privacy rights, the benefits of autonomous vehicles, and the environmental impact of green transportation solutions.

Connecting with the Book's Themes and Contributions

This vision for a sustainable and secure transportation system aligns closely with the themes explored throughout this book. In earlier chapters, we have discussed the role of FL in enhancing privacy and enabling intelligent decision-making in ITS. We have also seen how integrating advanced technologies such as 6G, blockchain, and edge intelligence can address many of the challenges faced by ITS. By integrating these technologies, the transportation system of the future will be smarter, safer, more efficient, and more sustainable.

The book's central theme of FL's potential for creating privacy-preserving and efficient transportation models finds its culmination in this vision for the future. The successful integration of FL with emerging paradigms such as 6G, blockchain, and edge intelligence offers a pathway toward achieving the goals of zero emissions, zero accidents, and zero trust gaps. Ultimately, the vision outlined here presents an ecosystem where ITS are self-organizing, resource-efficient, and capable of adapting to real-time changes, ensuring a safer and more sustainable future for all.

In conclusion, the future of transportation is not only about adopting new technologies but also about integrating privacy, security, and sustainability into the very fabric of ITS. This vision calls for a concerted effort from all stakeholders, guided by clear policies, ethical standards, and technical innovations. Achieving this vision will not only improve the efficiency of transportation systems but will also contribute to a greener, safer, and more equitable society [3].

Summary

This book provides a comprehensive exploration of FL in the context of smart mobility systems, emphasizing the significant role of FL in enhancing the safety, efficiency, and sustainability of ITS. From theoretical foundations to real-world applications, the book unfolds a logical progression from understanding the core principles of FL, to analyzing its specific applications in smart mobility, and finally to addressing the key challenges and future directions that shape the integration of FL into future transportation systems.

In the first chapter, *Introduction to FL for Smart Mobility*, we establish the foundational concept of FL and its relevance to the smart mobility landscape. The chapter outlines the inherent advantages of decentralized learning, focusing on data privacy and security, which are crucial in the context of smart mobility systems that collect and process sensitive data, such as vehicle locations, traffic conditions, and driver behaviors. FL offers a paradigm that respects user privacy while enabling collaborative model training, an essential feature in large-scale ITS applications.

The second chapter, *Foundations of FL and IoT Systems*, provides a deeper dive into the technical principles behind FL and its integration with IoT systems, which form the backbone of smart mobility infrastructure. We explore various FL architectures, including Horizontal, Vertical, and Hybrid FL, highlighting their respective advantages and limitations. The chapter establishes how FL can be leveraged to enhance IoT systems, enabling them to process vast amounts of data in a decentralized, efficient, and privacy-preserving manner, making it well-suited for applications like real-time traffic monitoring and V2V communication.

In *FL Applications in Smart Mobility*, the third chapter, we focus on how FL can be applied in real-world smart mobility scenarios, from AD to TFP and intelligent signal control. The chapter showcases several case studies where FL has been successfully deployed to improve operational efficiency, reduce congestion, and enhance safety in ITS. By leveraging FL, these systems can adapt to evolving traffic conditions, optimize resource usage, and ensure the secure sharing of data among multiple stakeholders.

The fourth chapter, *Case Studies and Research Insights*, builds upon the theoretical and practical knowledge introduced earlier, providing an in-depth analysis of research findings and case studies that demonstrate the tangible benefits and challenges of implementing FL in smart mobility systems. These insights provide valuable lessons on the deployment, scalability, and performance of FL in diverse ITS applications, such as vehicle autonomy, route recommendation, and congestion management.

Finally, *Challenges and Future Directions* addresses the key obstacles and potential future advancements in the integration of FL with smart mobility systems. We examine the current limitations, such as data heterogeneity, communication overhead, and system scalability, and provide insights into how future research and technological innovations—such as 6G, blockchain, and edge intelligence—can overcome these challenges. The chapter emphasizes the need for continued development in both the technical and policy aspects of FL to ensure its sustainable and effective use in ITS.

Throughout this book, we have illustrated how FL can transform smart mobility systems by providing a scalable, secure, and privacy-preserving framework for distributed data processing. By focusing on safety, efficiency, and sustainability, FL has the potential to significantly contribute to the development of next-generation transportation systems. The discussions and case studies presented offer valuable insights for both academic research and practical engineering implementations, highlighting the growing importance of FL in shaping the future of smart cities and ITS.

The value of this book lies not only in its comprehensive overview of the intersection between FL and smart mobility but also in its timely exploration of emerging challenges and opportunities in this rapidly evolving field. The insights and frameworks presented herein are essential for guiding future academic research and providing a roadmap for the successful deployment of FL in real-world smart mobility applications.

References

1. Abadi, M., Chu, A., Goodfellow, I., McMahan, H.B., Mironov, I., Talwar, K., Zhang, L.: Deep learning with differential privacy. In: Proceedings of the 2016 ACM SIGSAC Conference on Computer and Communications Security, pp 308–318 (2016)
2. Anderson, J.M., Nidhi, K., Stanley, K.D., Sorensen, P., Samaras, C., Oluwatola, O.A.: Autonomous Vehicle Technology: A Guide for Policymakers. Rand Corporation (2014)
3. Banister, D.: The sustainable mobility paradigm. Transp. policy **15**(2), 73–80 (2008)
4. Barocas, S., Selbst, A.D.: Big data's disparate impact. Calif. L Rev. **104**, 671 (2016)
5. Bradford, A.: The Brussels Effect: How the European Union Rules the World. Oxford University Press (2020)
6. Brown, T., Mann, B., Ryder, N., Subbiah, M., Kaplan, J.D., Dhariwal, P., Neelakantan, A., Shyam, P., Sastry, G., Askell, A., et al.: Language models are few-shot learners. Adv. Neural. Inf. Process. Syst. **33**, 1877–1901 (2020)
7. Caldas, S., Duddu, S.M.K., Wu, P., Li, T., Konečný, J., McMahan, H.B., Smith, V., Talwalkar, A.: Leaf: A benchmark for federated settings (2018). arXiv:1812.01097
8. Calo, R.: Robotics and the lessons of cyberlaw. Calif. L Rev. **103**, 513 (2015)
9. Cath, C., Wachter, S., Mittelstadt, B., Taddeo, M., Floridi, L.: Artificial intelligence and the 'good society': the us, eu, and uk approach. Sci. Eng. Ethics **24**(2), 505–528 (2018)
10. Chen, Y., Ning, Y., Slawski, M., Rangwala, H.: Asynchronous online federated learning for edge devices with non-iid data. In: 2020 IEEE International Conference on Big Data (Big Data), pp. 15–24. IEEE (2020)
11. Cruz, P., Achir, N., Viana, A.C.: On the edge of the deployment: a survey on multi-access edge computing. ACM Comput. Surv. **55**(5), 1–34 (2022)
12. Dresner, K., Stone, P.: Multiagent traffic management: a reservation-based intersection control mechanism. In: Autonomous Agents and Multiagent Systems, International Joint Conference on, IEEE Computer Society, vol. 3, pp. 530–537 (2004)
13. Dwork, C., Hardt, M., Pitassi, T., Reingold, O., Zemel, R.: Fairness through awareness. In: Proceedings of the 3rd Innovations in Theoretical Computer Science Conference, pp. 214–226 (2012)
14. Fagnant, D.J., Kockelman, K.: Preparing a nation for autonomous vehicles: opportunities, barriers and policy recommendations. Transp. Res. Part A: Policy Practice **77**, 167–181 (2015)
15. Fallah, A., Mokhtari, A., Ozdaglar, A.: Personalized federated learning with theoretical guarantees: a model-agnostic meta-learning approach. Adv. Neural. Inf. Process. Syst. **33**, 3557–3568 (2020)
16. Fereidooni, H., Marchal, S., Miettinen, M., Mirhoseini, A., Möllering, H., Nguyen, T.D., Rieger, P., Sadeghi, A.R., Schneider, T., Yalame, H., et al.: Safelearn: Secure aggregation for private federated learning. In: 2021 IEEE Security and Privacy Workshops (SPW), pp. 56–62. IEEE (2021)
17. Floridi, L., Cowls, J., Beltrametti, M., Chatila, R., Chazerand, P., Dignum, V., Luetge, C., Madelin, R., Pagallo, U., Rossi, F., et al.: Ai4people-an ethical framework for a good ai society: opportunities, risks, principles, and recommendations. Mind. Mach. **28**(4), 689–707 (2018)
18. Frankle, J., Carbin, M.: The lottery ticket hypothesis: finding sparse, trainable neural networks (2018). arXiv:1803.03635
19. Gebru, T., Morgenstern, J., Vecchione, B., Vaughan, J.W., Wallach, H., Iii, H.D., Crawford, K.: Datasheets for datasets. Commun. ACM **64**(12), 86–92 (2021)
20. Geels, F.W.: A socio-technical analysis of low-carbon transitions: introducing the multi-level perspective into transport studies. J. Transp. Geogr. **24**, 471–482 (2012)
21. Gentry, C.: Fully homomorphic encryption using ideal lattices. In: Proceedings of the Forty-First Annual ACM Symposium on Theory of Computing, pp. 169–178 (2009)
22. Goodman, B., Flaxman, S.: European union regulations on algorithmic decision-making and a "right to explanation." AI Mag. **38**(3), 50–57 (2017)
23. Grieves, M.: Digital twin: manufacturing excellence through virtual factory replication. White Pap. **1**(2014), 1–7 (2014)

24. Hodge, G.A.: Reviewing public-private partnerships: some thoughts on evaluation. In: International Handbook on Public-Private Partnerships. Edward Elgar Publishing (2010)
25. Janssen, M., Brous, P., Estevez, E., Barbosa, L.S., Janowski, T.: Data governance: organizing data for trustworthy artificial intelligence. Gov. Inf. Q. **37**(3), 101493 (2020)
26. Kindervag, J., et al.: Build security into your network's dna: the zero trust network architecture. Forrester Res. Inc. **27**, 1–16 (2010)
27. Lai, F., Zhu, X., Madhyastha, H.V., Chowdhury, M.: Oort: efficient federated learning via guided participant selection. In: 15th USENIX Symposium on Operating Systems Design and Implementation (OSDI 21), pp. 19–35 (2021)
28. Li, Q., Diao, Y., Chen, Q., He, B.: Federated learning on non-iid data silos: an experimental study. In: 2022 IEEE 38th International Conference on Data Engineering (ICDE), pp. 965–978. IEEE (2022)
29. Li, T., Sahu, A.K., Zaheer, M., Sanjabi, M., Talwalkar, A., Smith, V.: Federated optimization in heterogeneous networks. Proc. Mach. Learn. Syst. **2**, 429–450 (2020)
30. Lim, W.Y.B., Luong, N.C., Hoang, D.T., Jiao, Y., Liang, Y.C., Yang, Q., Niyato, D., Miao, C.: Federated learning in mobile edge networks: a comprehensive survey. IEEE Commun. Surv. Tutorials **22**(3), 2031–2063 (2020)
31. Lin, Y., Han, S., Mao, H., Wang, Y., Dally, W.J.: Deep gradient compression: Reducing the communication bandwidth for distributed training (2017). arXiv:1712.01887
32. Marchant, G.E.: The growing gap between emerging technologies and the law. In: The Growing Gap Between Emerging Technologies and Legal-Ethical Oversight: The Pacing Problem, pp. 19–33 (2011)
33. Mehrabi, N., Morstatter, F., Saxena, N., Lerman, K., Galstyan, A.: A survey on bias and fairness in machine learning. ACM Comput. Surv. (CSUR) **54**(6), 1–35 (2021)
34. Melis, L., Song, C., De Cristofaro, E., Shmatikov, V.: Exploiting unintended feature leakage in collaborative learning. In: 2019 IEEE Symposium on Security and Privacy (SP), pp. 691–706. IEEE (2019)
35. Mothukuri, V., Parizi, R.M., Pouriyeh, S., Huang, Y., Dehghantanha, A., Srivastava, G.: A survey on security and privacy of federated learning. Future Gener. Comput. Syst. **115**, 619–640 (2021)
36. Nishio, T., Yonetani, R.: Client selection for federated learning with heterogeneous resources in mobile edge. In: ICC 2019-2019 IEEE International Conference on Communications (ICC), pp. 1–7. IEEE (2019)
37. Pardau, S.L.: The california consumer privacy act: Towards a european-style privacy regime in the united states. J. Tech. L Pol'y **23**, 68 (2018)
38. Protection, F.D.: General data protection regulation (gdpr). Intersoft Consult. **24**(1) (2018). Accessed in October
39. Qu, Y., Uddin, M.P., Gan, C., Xiang, Y., Gao, L., Yearwood, J.: Blockchain-enabled federated learning: a survey. ACM Comput. Surv. **55**(4), 1–35 (2022)
40. Radford, A., Wu, J., Child, R., Luan, D., Amodei, D., Sutskever, I., et al.: Language models are unsupervised multitask learners. OpenAI Blog **1**(8), 9 (2019)
41. Reddi, S., Charles, Z., Zaheer, M., Garrett, Z., Rush, K., Konečný, J., Kumar, S., McMahan, H.B.: Adaptive federated optimization (2020). arXiv:2003.00295
42. Rosen, R., Von Wichert, G., Lo, G., Bettenhausen, K.D.: About the importance of autonomy and digital twins for the future of manufacturing. Ifac-Papersonline **48**(3), 567–572 (2015)
43. Rowe, G., Frewer, L.J.: Evaluating public-participation exercises: a research agenda. Sci. Technol. Human Values **29**(4), 512–556 (2004)
44. Rudin, C.: Stop explaining black box machine learning models for high stakes decisions and use interpretable models instead. Nat. Mach. Intell. **1**(5), 206–215 (2019)
45. Samarakoon, N., Herath, D., Sankalpa, K., Sampath, S., Wickramasingha, M.: A comprehensive review of electric vehicles. J. Res. Technol. Eng. **5**(03), 111–142 (2024)
46. Satyanarayanan, M.: The emergence of edge computing. Computer **50**(1), 30–39 (2017)
47. Shokri, R., Shmatikov, V.: Privacy-preserving deep learning. In: Proceedings of the 22nd ACM SIGSAC Conference on Computer and Communications Security, pp. 1310–1321 (2015)

48. Tanuwidjaja, H.C., Choi, R., Baek, S., Kim, K.: Privacy-preserving deep learning on machine learning as a service—a comprehensive survey. IEEE Access **8**, 167425–167447 (2020)
49. Tataria, H., Shafi, M., Molisch, A.F., Dohler, M., Sjöland, H., Tufvesson, F.: 6g wireless systems: vision, requirements, challenges, insights, and opportunities. Proc. IEEE **109**(7), 1166–1199 (2021)
50. Tolpegin, V., Truex, S., Gursoy, M.E., Liu, L.: Data poisoning attacks against federated learning systems. In: European Symposium on Research in Computer Security, pp. 480–501, Springer, Berlin (2020)
51. Wachter, S., Mittelstadt, B., Floridi, L.: Why a right to explanation of automated decision-making does not exist in the general data protection regulation. Int. Data Privacy Law **7**(2), 76–99 (2017)
52. Yao, A.C.: Protocols for secure computations. In: 23rd Annual Symposium on Foundations of Computer Science (sfcs 1982), pp. 160–164. IEEE (1982)
53. Zhang, T., Mao, S.: An introduction to the federated learning standard. GetMobile: Mobile Comput. Commun. **25**(3), 18–22 (2022)
54. Zhu, C., Leung, V.C., Shu, L., Ngai, E.C.H.: Green internet of things for smart world. IEEE Access **3**, 2151–2162 (2015)

MIX
Papier aus verantwortungsvollen Quellen
Paper from responsible sources
FSC® C105338

If you have any concerns about our products,
you can contact us on
ProductSafety@springernature.com

In case Publisher is established outside the EU,
the EU authorized representative is:
Springer Nature Customer Service Center GmbH
Europaplatz 3, 69115 Heidelberg, Germany

Printed by Libri Plureos GmbH
in Hamburg, Germany